AYATULLAH IBRAHIM AMINI

Principles of Marriage and Family Ethics

First published by Islamic Propagation Organization 1997

Copyright © 1997 by Ayatullah Ibrahim Amini

All rights reserved. No part of this publication may be reproduced, stored or transmitted in any form or by any means, electronic, mechanical, photocopying, recording, scanning, or otherwise without written permission from the publisher. It is illegal to copy this book, post it to a website, or distribute it by any other means without permission.

First edition

Contents

Foreword	1
Preface	3
Part 1: The Duties of Women	8
The Purpose of Marriage	8
Living with Husband	12
Kindness	14
The Husband's Respect	16
Complaints and Grievances	18
Pleasant Dispositions	20
Wrong Expectations	23
Be a Comfort for Your Husband	25
Be Appreciative	27
Do not Look for Shortcomings	29
Don't Look at Anyone Other Than Your Husband	32
Islamic Hijab	33
Forgive Your Husband's Mistakes	37
Coping with Your Husband's Relatives	38
Coping With Your Husband's Job	40
If You Have to Live Away From Your Hometown	43
If Your Husband Works at Home	45
Help Your Husband to Make Progress	47
Be Careful That He is Not Misled	48
Suspicious Women	52
Do Not Pay Attention to Slanderous Talks	63

The Satisfaction of Your Husband and Not Your Mother	66
Be Clean and Beautiful at Home Also	70
Be a Mother to Him	72
Keep the Secrets	73
Accept His Management	74
Be Resourceful when Times are Hard	76
Do not Refuse to Talk and do not Sulk	78
Remain Silent when he is Angry	81
Men's Hobbies	83
Housekeeping	83
Cleanliness	85
A Tidy House	89
Preparing Food	92
Receiving Guests	96
The Trustee of the House	101
Careers of women	103
Do not Waste your Spare Time	107
Motherhood (Caring for Children)	109
Fruit of Marriage	109
Educating a Child	110
Nutrition and Hygiene	112
Part 2: The Duties of Men	116
The Guardian of the Family	116
Taking Care of your Wife	117
Be Loving towards Her	118
Respect Your Wife	121
Be Well-mannered	123
Complaining Unnecessarily	128
Picking up Quarrels	130
Appease Her and Sympathize with Her	132
Do not pick up Faults	133

Do not Pay Attention to Slanderous Talk of the Critics	135
Overlook Her Mistakes	140
Be Attentive	147
The Disciplinary Rights of the Husband	151
Suspicious Men	156
The Unfaithful Woman	162
Do not Go After Other Women	164
Be Grateful	167
Be Clean at Home Also	169
Nurse Your Wife	171
Family Economy	173
Extend Your Help in the Household Works	176
Return Home Soon	177
Be Faithful	178
Education and Training	180
Having A Child	183
Pregnancy and Childbirth	190
Assistance in Bringing up Children	193
The Major Obstacle in Settling down Disagreements	194
Divorce	196

Foreword

The human society is comprised of families. Islam attaches great importance to real pleasure and prosperity of human beings through Islamically balanced, highly ethical, well-educated and well- behaved families and happy homes. Like in all the elds of human activity, Islam has laid down clearly and in detail the rights and duties of men and women, husbands and wives and also parents and children. The happy homes having pleasant environment, in which husband, wife, children and other relatives live together merrily with good mutual understanding, tolerance and respect as well as fullling their respective duties towards each other, is indeed an index of the highest status the Almighty Allah has blessed, among the creatures, to all human beings.

Unfortunately, the lack of appreciation about these aspects, particularly by husbands and wives, leads to many problems for themselves as well as for the children-the future generations. In advanced and western countries, with more and more progress, greater technological and scientic achievements and very fast and ultramodern way of life, the rate of divorces and separations is alarming.

Considering the importance of the subject, the I.P.O. is taking the privilege of publishing this book (originally in Persian language) written by an eminent Islamic scholar, a noted author and a senior professor of Islamic Jurisprudence at, *Hawzah Ilmiyyah* (Islamic Theological Centre), Qum, Iran, Hujjatul-Islam Ibrahim Amini.

The author has taken great pains in conducting research and deep study on the subject of family ethics and husband-wife relationship. The rst part deals with duties of women and the second part contains duties of men. Along with the duties, rights of husbands on wives and those of wives on husbands have also been described quoting relevant verses of the Holy Qur'an and *Ahadith* (traditions).

It is hoped that the book would be found very useful for all and every home would treasure this to derive the maximum benet for creating and maintaining the serene and pleasant environment, full of Allah's blessings.

International Relations Department Islamic Propagation Organization

Preface

The greatest desire of all young men and women who reach the age of puberty is to marry. Through the establishment of a joint marital life, they would earn more independence, as well as have a kind and trustworthy partner. They regard marriage as the beginning of their lives of prosperity.

Man has been created for woman and *vice versa*.

They are attracted to each other like magnets. Marriage and establishing a joint life is a natural desire of human beings responding to their instincts. It is considered one of the greatest Divine blessings. In fact, where else could one nd a better shelter for the youth than a sincere family unit?

It is the desire of raising a family which preserves the youth from pursuing irrational dreams and internal anxieties. The marital union enables them to nd a kind and faithful partner who could share the hard and difcult times. The sacred marital covenant is a Divine rope which links the hearts, calms them when they become unsettled, and focuses irrational dreams on one ideal goal. The house is the centre of love, kindness, and friendship, whereby it is the best place to relax and live comfortably.

The Almighty Allah mentions this blessing in the Holy Qur'an:

"And one of His signs is that He created mates for you from yourselves that you may nd rest in them and He put between you love and compassion; most surely there are signs in this for a people who reect" (The Holy Qur'an, 30:21).

"The Prophet (S) of Islam stated: 'A man who is not married, even though he may be wealthy is surely poor and needy: and the same is true for a woman.'"[1]

"Imam as-Sadiq (a.s.) asked a man: 'Are you married?" The man replied "no". The Imam stated: 'I would not like to stay unmarried even for one night, even if I were to own the whole world.'"[2]

"The Holy Prophet (S) stated: 'There has not been created any institution in Islam which is more favored and dearer to Allah than marriage.'"[3]

Even though the Compassionate Allah has endowed human beings with such a precious blessing, they do not appreciate it and sometimes due to ignorance and selshness, convert this warm and blessed union, into a dark prison or even a burning Hell! It is due to man's own ignorance that the members of the family have to live in this dark prison or that the sacred marital covenant has to be destroyed.

If a couple is aware of their duties and acts accordingly, then a house would be a place of friendship and would resemble heaven. But, if there are family differences and arguments, the family home, could truly change into a prison. Family differences are due to various reasons, such as economic factors, family background of the man and woman,

---

[1] Wasa 'il al Shiah, vol. 14, p 3.

[2] Ibid.

[3] Ibid, p 23

living environment, unwanted interference by fathers, mothers and relatives, and tens of other reasons.

But according to the author, the most important factor is the ignorance of husband and wife regarding their duties and lack of preparation for their marital life. Generally, in order to accomplish a task, expertise and readiness are necessary requirements. If one lacks the necessary knowledge and readiness, then one cannot successfully achieve his desired goal. Thus, training classes are formed to educate people for different tasks.

Expertise, readiness, and knowledge are also needed in marriage. A young man must possess enough information about his wife's principles of values and internal desires. He must also be aware of marital problems and ways of solving them. He should not regard marriage as merely buying goods, or hiring a maid, but to acknowledge it as a treaty of friendship, honesty, kindness, partnership, and cooperation in a joint family life.

A young woman should also be aware of her husband's philosophy of life and wishes. She should not consider that marriage is like engaging a servant for fullling needs without any terms and conditions; but as a pledge for partnership and cooperation in making efforts for conducting the life. In order to obtain a successful partnership, there is a need for understanding, cooperation, and devotion.

Although the future of young men and women largely depends on a marriage which requires awareness of the importance of the concepts of marriage and preparation for undertaking such a task, our society unfortunately neglects the importance of these conditions.

The parents pay a great deal of attention to such points as dowry, beauty, and personality. However, they disregard the readiness for establishing a marital life as a necessary condition. They marry their sons and daughters off without providing adequate information about family life.

Consequently two young and inexperienced people step into a new life and confront many problems. Differences, arguments, and ghts begin to develop. Their parents then interfere to help resolve the differences. But, since their interferences are mostly biased, the differences are exaggerated and the situation becomes worse.

The initial years of family life are eventful and critical. This is the period where many families can be torn between divorce and disintegration. Some of them continue their marriage and prefer this self-made prison to divorce and others learn more about each other and form a relatively comfortable life.

What a nice thing it could be had there been some means of educating and informing young men and women about the foundations and the establishment of marriage in the form of classes entitled "marriage preparation" which would prepare them for establishing their own families. I am hopeful of the day that such program is established.

The present book is written on the basis of this necessity. In resolving the issues of this book, I have relied upon the Holy Qur'an, the traditions of the Holy Prophet (S) and the Infallible Imams (a.s.), as well as some general statistics, and my personal experience.

Although certain guidelines for a better marriage have been presented, I do not claim that all family problems can be solved by reading this book. It is hoped that the book will provide better insight and awareness for those experiencing marital and family problems. It is highly expected of those responsible' persons who realize the importance of this matter, to take serious steps in order to help those who suffer from the agonies and sufferings of family deterioration and conict. (Insha'Allah)

This book has been divided in two parts. The rst part concerns the duties of women to their husbands and the second part covers the duties of men to their wives. But men and women are recommended to read both parts in order to get a better insight into the matter. By reading only one part of the book, the reader might feel a bias towards one side or the other; but by reading both the parts, one would admit that this is not the case.

Ibrahim Amini Qum
July 1975

Part 1: The Duties of Women

The Purpose of Marriage

Marriage is a natural necessity for every human being. It bears many good outcomes of which the most important ones are:

1. The formation of a family through which one can nd security and peace of mind. A person who is not married resembles a bird without a nest. Marriage serves as a shelter for anyone who feels lost in the wilderness of life; one can nd a partner in life who would share one's joy and sorrow.

2. The natural sexual desire is both strong and signicant. Everyone should have a partner for satisfying their sexual needs in a secure and serene environment. Everyone should enjoy sexual satisfaction in a correct and proper manner. Those who abstain from marriage often suffer from both physical and psychological disorders. Such disorders and certain social problems are a direct consequence of the abstinence of youth from marriage.

3. Reproduction: Through marriage the procreation of mankind is continued. Children are the result of marriage and are important factors in stabilizing the family foundations as well as a source of real joy to their parents.

A great deal of emphasis has been given in the Holy Qur'an and the Traditions to both marriage and having children. The Almighty Allah states in the Holy Qur'an:

> *"And among His signs is this, that He created for you mates from among yourselves..." (The Holy Qur'an, 30:21).*

"The Prophet (S) stated: 'There is no better structure founded in Islam other than marriage.'"[4]

"Imam Ali (a.s) stated: 'Engage in marriage; because this is the tradition of the Prophet (S) of Allah.'"[5]

"The Prophet of Allah (swt) stated: 'Whoever chooses to follow my tradition must get married and produce offspring through marriage (and increase the population of Muslims) so that on the day of resurrection I shall confront other Ummah (nations) with the (great) numbers of my Ummah.'"[6]

"Imam Rida (a.s) stated: 'The greatest gain for a man is a faithful woman who, when she sees him, becomes happy and protects his property and her own honor in his absence.'"[7]

What has been dealt with so far in this chapter has been only the

---

[4] Wasa 'il al Shiah, vol 14, p 3.

[5] Ibid

[6] Ibid

[7] Ibid, p 23

worldly and animalistic side of marriage which the animals also share: the Benets of companionship and reproduction. As such the true purpose of marriage for the human race is of a different kind. Mankind is not meant to have entered this world solely in order to eat, drink, sleep, seek pleasure or act lustfully, and then to die and be destroyed.

The status of man is higher than such deeds. Human beings are meant to train themselves and their souls by gaining knowledge, committing good deeds, and behaving with good manners. Man is meant to take steps along the straight path to achieve nearness to Almighty Allah. Mankind is a creation that is able to cleanse his soul and by avoiding evil deeds and exercising good behavior reach a level of such high status that even the angels are not able to attain. Man is a creature that is eternal. He has come to this world so that by the guidance of the prophets and the implementation of the programs set by the religion (of Islam), to secure his happiness in this world and the Hereafter; so that he could live a peaceful life in the next world eternally.

Therefore, the purpose of marriage should be searched for in this spiritual context. The aim of marriage for a religious person should be a means of avoiding evil deeds and purging one's soul of sins. It should be a means of acquiring nearness to the Almighty Allah. It is in this context that a suitable and good partner assumes an important role. When two believers, through marriage, form a family, their sexual relationship would benet them in strengthening their mutual love and kindness, for such a couple, there would not exist any dangerous threats of sexual perversion, dangerous addictions or unlawful deeds.

The Prophet (S) of Islam and all of the Imams (a.s) have laid great emphasis on the institution of marriage.

"The Prophet (S) stated: 'Whoever gets married, has safeguarded half of his religion.'"[8]

---

[8] Ibid, p 5

"Imam as-Sadiq (a.s.) stated: 'Two Rak'ats (units) of a married person's Salat (prayer) are better than seventy Rak'ats offered by a bachelor.'"9

A faithful, pious, and harmonious partner plays a crucial role in having a respectable and honest life. Indeed having such a partner is an important factor when wanting to avoid evil deeds and enables the commitment of oneself in performing the obligatory acts of worship. A pious couple, not only would not meet with any obstacle in achieving religious goals, but would be a source of encouragement to each other.

Is it really possible for a faithful man of Allah to gloriously ght in His way, without the approval of his wife? Is it possible for any pious person to earn his living lawfully, observing all religious aspects, paying statutory religious alms to avoid extravagance, and to spend on charitable deeds without the consent of his wife?

A pious person would always invite his partner to goodness, just as a corrupt person would tempt his partner towards corruption. It is then reasonable that, in Islam men and women, who want to get married, are advised to regard the piety and good manners of their future partners, as essential conditions.

"The Prophet (S) stated: 'If I were to bestow all the good of both worlds upon a Muslim person, I would endow him with a humble heart, a tongue which continuously utters his praises, a body patient enough to withstand all calamities; and I would give him a pious spouse who, when she sees him, becomes happy, and protects his property and her own honor in his absence.'"10

"One person went to the Prophet (S) and said: 'I have a wife who always welcomes me when I come home, and escorts me to the door when I leave. When she nds me sad and unhappy, she then, by consoling

---

[9] Ibid, p 6

[10] Ibid, p 23

me says: 'If you are thinking of sustenance, then do not despair, because Allah provides sustenance; and if you are thinking about the next life, then may Allah increase your intellect and efforts. Then the Prophet (S) stated: ' Allah surely has functionaries and agents in this world and your wife is one of those. Such a woman would be rewarded half as much as a martyr.'"[11]

"Imam Ali (a.s) was thinking the same when he spoke of Hadrat Zahra (a.s). He stated that she was the best help for worshipping the Almighty Allah. History tells us that the Prophet (S), one day after the wedding of Imam Ali (a.s) and Hadrat Zahra (a.s), went to congratulate them in their house and know about their welfare. He asked Imam Ali (a.s): 'How do you nd your spouse?' The Imam replied: 'I found Zahra as the best help in worshipping the Almighty Allah.' The Prophet (S) then asked the same of Zahra (a.s), and she replied: 'He is the best husband.'"[12]

Imam Ali (a.s), in one sentence, introduced the best woman in Islam and expressed the main purpose of marriage.

Living with Husband

The task of a wife is to maintain and take care of a husband. It is not an easy undertaking. Those women, who are unaware of this feature of their role, may nd difculty in fullling the task. It is a job for the woman who is aware that the job requires a degree of sagacity, style, and ingenuity. For a woman to be a successful wife, she should win over her husband's heart and be a source of comfort to him.

She should encourage him to do good deeds while dissuading him from bad ones. She should also provide adequate measures to maintain his health and well-being. The results of her efforts are directed

---

[11] Ibid, p 17

[12] Bihar al-Anwar, vol 43, p 117

towards making the man into a kind and respected husband who would be a proper guardian for his family, and a good father from whom the children would seek guidance and respect. Allah, the All- Knowing has endowed woman with extraordinary power. The prosperity and happiness as well as the misery of the family are in her hands.

A woman can turn the home into a lofty paradise or a burning hell. She can lead her husband to the peak of success or the dregs of misfortune. The woman with the qualities bestowed on her by Allah, who is aware of her role as a spouse, can elevate her husband to a respected man even if he had been the lowest of all men.

"One learned scholar wrote: 'Women possess a strange power in that they are able to acquire whatever they desire.'"[13]

In Islam, taking care of one's husband has an important position. It has been equated to the role of Jihad (holy war in the path of Allah). "Imam Ali (a.s) stated: 'The *Jihad* of a woman is to take care of her husband well.'"[14]

Considering that *Jihad* is the struggle and holy war in the path of Allah including the struggle for advancement and honor of Islam, defending the Islamic territories and execution of social justice, it is one of the highest acts of worship. The value of fullling the duties of a proper spouse is also reected upon when considering *Jihad*.

"The Prophet (S) of Islam stated: ' Any woman who dies while her husband is pleased with her, enters Paradise.'"[15]

The Holy Prophet also stated: "If a woman does not perform her duty as a spouse, she has not done her duty to Allah.'"[16]

---

[13] Dar Aghushe Khushakhfi, p 142

[14] Bihar al-Anwar, vol 103, p 254

[15] Mahajjat al-Bayda, vol 2, p 70

[16] Mustadrak, vol 2, p 552

Kindness

Everyone is thirsty for friendship and kindness; They all like to be loved by others. The heart of a human being thrives on it. A person who is not loved by anyone regards himself as alone and deserted. Dear lady! Your husband is not any different. He is also in need of love and affection. Before his marriage the love and affection of his parents fullled this need, but now, he expects you to fulll it.

The man looks towards his spouse to nd friendship and love, which is a requirement of all human beings. He struggles hard to earn a living and to comfort you. He shares with you all the hardships of life and as your true partner cares for your happiness even more than your parents. Therefore, express your appreciation to him and love him, he will love you. Love is a two-way relationship which unites the hearts.

A twenty-year old boy who had come to Tehran to study at the university fell in love with a 39-year old widow who was his landlady. This was because the woman had fullled the empty place of his mother in his heart through her kindness.[17]

If love is mutual, the marital foundation becomes strong and the dangers of separation are averted. Do not proudly think that your husband fell in love with you at rst sight, because such love is not lasting. A lasting love is through kindness and permanent affection in the form of a very close friendship.

If you love your husband and have a good friendship he will be happy and willing to strive and sacrice himself for your well-being. A man who enjoys the love of his wife, rarely suffers from poor health or has emotional problems. If a man is deprived of a warm and friendly

---

[17] Ittela'at, 20th Esfand, 1348 Solar Hijri*, no. 13140. *By Solar Hijri is meant Solar Calendar based on Hijrah of Prophet Muhammad (SA). Difference between the Gregorian calendar and Solar Hijri is 621 years.

relationship with his spouse, he may become disheartened and may avoid his home. He may end up spending a great deal of time out of his home in search of friends and attention. He may say to himself: "Why should I work and support the people who do not like me. I might as well enjoy myself and try to nd genuine friends."

A woman may sincerely love her husband, but does not show it or express it very often. It is not enough to establish the ties of friendship and take it for granted. Occasional expressions of statements such a "I love you," "I missed you," "I am happy to see you," help enormously in promoting a good relationship.

When the husband is on a trip, the woman should write letters expressing that she missed him. If there is a telephone at the man's ofce, the wife should phone him occasionally, but not in excess. She should praise him among friends and relatives when he is absent, and defend him if anyone is talking against him.

The Almighty Allah refers to this bond of love and affection of a husband and wife in the Qur'an:

> ***"And one of His signs is that He created mates for you from yourselves that you may nd rest in them, and He put between you love and compassion; most surely there are signs in this for a people who reect." (The Holy Qur'an, 30:21).***

"Imam Rida (a.s) stated: 'Some women are blessings for their husbands who express their love and affection.'"[18]

"The Holy Prophet (S) stated: 'The best of you among women are those who possess love and affection.'"[19]

---

[18] Mustadrak, vol 2, p 532

[19] Bihar al-Anwar, vol 103, p 235

"Imam as-Sadiq (a.s.) stated: 'When you love someone, let the person know.'"[20]

The Husband's Respect

The desire for respect is an inherent one, but not everyone is willing to give it readily. Your husband is in contact with many people during the day while away from home. Some may be impolite and insulting him which eventually can upset the person. As his wife, he expects you to show respect and encouragement at home and thereby boost his trampled ego.

To honor and respect your husband does not belittle you, but it provides energy and inclination to struggle to make a better life. You should always greet him, and with your greeting, give him a feeling of veneration. Do not interrupt him when he is talking. Be courteous and polite when you are talking to him and do not shout at him. Let him enter rst when both of you are going to a meeting.

Praise him in front of others. Ask your children to respect him and reprimand them if they are discourteous towards him. Be respectful of him in front of guests and be attentive to his needs, as well as the guests. When he is knocking at the door you should try to open the door with a smile and a happy expression. This small act of happiness has such an effect that it refreshes the man's tired spirits. Some women may think that such behaviour is strange. Imagine greeting your husband as if he was a guest.

This is not the correct attitude because the man has been struggling all the day for the well-being of his family and he deserves some consideration and respect when he returns home. That rst greeting makes a big impression and what's good for a guest is good for the

---

[20] Ibid, vol 74, p 181

family members.

"The Holy Prophet (S) stated: 'The duty of a woman is to answer the call at the door and welcome her husband.'"[21]

"Imam as-Sadiq (a.s.) stated: 'A woman who respects her husband and does not harass him, will be fortunate and prosperous.'"[22]

"The Holy Prophet (S) stated: 'A wife is duty-bound to arrange for a basin and towel to wash her husband's hands.'"[23]

Be careful not to humiliate him, do not talk to him harshly, do not abuse him, do not be inattentive to him, and do not call him by any obscene titles. If you offend him, he, in turn, will insult you. Eventually, the spirit of love and trust will erode. Consequently, you will have constant quarrels and arguments which may lead to a divorce. Even if you continue to live together, your lives will surely be lled with many turbulent moments. Feelings of antagonism and psychological disturbances may build up to the point that it becomes hazardous to the couple's life in that it may lead to crime. The following stories, illustrate some of these points:

"A twenty-two year old man, stabbed his 19-year old wife to death after he was abused by her. In the court he said: 'I was married to this woman a year ago. At the beginning my wife loved me very much. But it was not long before she changed and started to humiliate me. She would use abusive language with me on every possible occasion and over the smallest issue, would make fun of me. Due to a squint in my left eye, she used to call me a "blind ass". One day she called me a "blind ass" and I became so furious that I stabbed her fteen times with a knife.'"[24]

---

[21] Mustadrak, vol 3, p 551

[22] Bihar al-Anwar, vol 103, p 253

[23] Mustadrak, vol 3, p 551

[24] Ittela'at, 14th Urdibahisht, 1351 Solar Hijri, no 13787

"A seventy-one year old man who had killed his wife, explained: 'Suddenly her manners towards me changed and she started to ignore me. Once she called me "an intolerable man". I realized that she did not love me any more; I became suspicious of her and killed her with two blows of an axe.'"[25]

Complaints and Grievances

There is not anyone who does not have problems and grievances with regard to daily life. Everyone likes to have a sympathetic person with whom he can conde and who will listen to his problems. But the point to remember is that "there is a time and place for everything". One should realize the proper time and occasion to complain. Some ignorant and selsh women do not realize that their husbands are very tired and nervous after a long day's work. Instead of waiting an hour or two for him to regain his spirits, they start attacking him with a barrage of complaints. For instance the wife may say:

"You have left me with these damned kids and rushed off. Ahmad has broken the glass in the door of the front room. Our daughters have been ghting. I am going crazy with the noise of the kids outside. Hasan does not study at all and he has secured poor marks. I have been working so hard today and I am exhausted. Nobody listens to my cries!

These kids don't help at all in the house-work. I wish I didn't have any children at all! By the way your sister was here today. I don't know what was wrong with her; she acted as if I had swallowed her father's inheritance. May God save me from your mother! She has been talking ill about me behind my back. I am fed up with all of them. Also, I cut my nger badly with a knife today.

I wish I'd not gone to Muhammad's wedding yesterday. You should

---

[25] Ibid, 1st Azar, 1350 Solar Hijri, no 13652

have seen Rashid's wife! What an outt! Allah should give me the same luck! Some men really love their wives and buy them beautiful things. They are real husbands. When Rashid entered, everybody respected him. It's true that people are only interested in what you're wearing. What has she got that I haven't? Why should she show off in front of me?! Oh yes, she is fortunate to have a husband who loves her, he isn't like you!

I can't stand this damned house any longer, looking after your and your children. So do what you like!"

This sort of attitude is incorrect. Women of this sort think that their husbands are going on a picnic or pleasure-ride every morning. Men confront hundreds of problems every day. Dear lady! you do not know what your husband has gone through when he is at work. You do not know what rude and obnoxious people he has had to deal with all the day. So, when he comes home, you should not present all of your complaints at the same time. He should not feel guilty of being a man. Be fair and be considerate to him. If you, by grumbling and nagging, add to his worries and anguish, then he may either start a row or just leave the house and go to a cafe, cinema, or even walk around the streets.

Therefore, dear lady! For the sake of Allah, give up this habit of complaining at inopportune moments. Find a suitable time and then present him with your genuine problems, not by complaining, but in a consultative type of way. In this way, you do not create antagonistic feelings in him and the family bonds remain secure

"The Prophet (S) of Islam stated: 'The prayers of a woman who teases her husband with her tongue, are not accepted (by Allah) even though she fasts every day, gets up for the acts of worship every night, sets free a few slaves and donates her wealth in the way of Allah. A bad-tongue woman who hurts her husband in this way, is the rst person who enters hell.'"26

"The Holy Prophet (S) also stated: 'The women of Paradise say to those women who abuse their husbands in this way: 'May Allah kill you. Do not misbehave with your husband. This man (the husband) is not yours, and you do not deserve him. Soon he will leave you and come towards us.'" 27

I do not know what such women want to achieve by their grumbling. If they want to attract their husband's attention or to show off, then surely they achieve the exact opposite and exasperate him. If they intend to distress him, to create for him psychological problems and to lead him towards fatal articial addictions, then they are on the right track.

Dear lady! if you care about your husband and your family, then you should give up this improper and illogical attitude. Have you ever thought that your misconduct may lead towards breaking up your family life?

"One doctor testied in court: 'I have not yet seen my wife act like a proper housewife during all my married life. Our house is always in a mess. She is always shouting and abusing. I am fed up with her'. After paying her a lump sum money, he received divorce. He said joyfully: 'If she had wanted and had asked for all my wealth and even my medical degree, I would have given it to get rid of her sooner.'"28

Pleasant Dispositions

Anyone who is good-natured with a pleasant disposition would also face the hardships and problems of life in the same manner. These are

---

[26] Bihar al-Anwar, vol 76, p 363

[27] Mahajjat al-Bayda, vol 2, p 72

[28] Ittela'at, 13th Dey, 1350 Solar Hijri, no 13689

the kinds of personality that people are attracted to and continually seek. The pleasant disposition and attitude of a person would be immune to psychological disorders since their outlook to life is to overcome their hardships in the best feasible manner.

"Imam as-Sadiq (a.s) stated: 'No life is more agreeable than the one which is of a pleasant nature.'"[29]

But an ill-natured person would likewise nd life unpleasant since the relationship of such people promote anxiety and tension. Such a person enjoys complaining and voicing one's dissonance with life. This type of attitude is avoided by most people whereby the person ends up with very few friends, these are then the conditions which are susceptible to various psychological problems, and other illnesses due to the anxiety and emptiness with which the person with a bad attitude views life.

"The Holy Prophet (S) stated: 'A person with a bad disposition and attitude would be in permanent agony and suffering.'"[30]

A good and pleasant attitude is essential between all people in general and between couples in particular since the couple must be together to form a joint life.

Dear lady! If you want to enjoy a pleasant life with your husband and children, make your attitude and disposition pleasant and agreeable. Be good-natured and not quarrelsome. You have the ability to turn your house into a lofty paradise or a burning hell. You can be an angel of mercy whereby your husband and children can nd peace through you. Do you know what a beautiful impression you would leave on their souls with your smiling attitude and good language? The pleasant impression is fresh in their minds as they start off to school or work and helps them to make a good start of the day.

---

[29] Bihar al-Anwar vol 71, p 389

[30] Ibid, vol 73, p 298

Therefore, if you care about the quality of your life and the relationship you have with your husband; do not be negative in nature. Be positive in your attitude and disposition since the best supportive pillar of security to marriage is a good set of ethics leading to a pleasant disposition.

Most instances of divorce are due to the incompatible nature of man and wife. The statistics on divorce conclusively indicate that the compatible attitude, moral values and disposition was non-existent in the couples. The main source of family rows and discord is due to the incompatible character of the couple's ethical principles and values. The following set of data is of interest:

"In the year 1968, 12,760 cases out of a total of 16,039 cases of marital complaints brought to court were based on incompatible moral foundations. In 1969, 11,246 cases out of a total of 16,058 cases, were based on the same reason. It is therefore evident that more than seventy per cent of family rows were due to this factor."[31]

"A woman complained to the Council that her husband always ate his lunch and dinner outside. The husband then explained that the reason he ate outside was because his wife had absolutely no constructiveness in her and she was the worst of all the ill-disposed women in the world. The wife suddenly got up and started beating her husband in front of the judges."[32]

This foolish woman thought that by complaining, abusing and beating, she could bring him back home. But she did not use the simple and intelligent method which was to be more considerate and to observe appropriate conduct.

"Another woman reported to the court that her husband has not been talking to her for 15 months and that he was paying for living

---

[31] Ittela'at, 15th Azar, 1350 Solar Hijri

[32] Ibid, 3rd Bahman, 1350 Solar Hijri

expenses through his mother. The husband replied that he had enough of his wife's ill-disposed attitude which made him decide not to talk to her for 15 months.'"[33]

Most of the family conicts may be resolved with kindness, compassion and a pleasant disposition. If your husband is unkind, if he goes out for dinners alone, if he is abusive, wastes away all his wealth, speaks of divorce and separation or a number of reasons for family conict, there is only one way to resolve them. The way is by being kind and good-natured. The results of exercising such behavior are miraculous.

"Imam as-Sadiq (a.s) stated: 'Allah Almighty will grant a well-disposed person a reward equivalent to the blessings of Jihad. He will endow many blessings onto him day and night.'"[34]

"Imam as-Sadiq (a.s.) stated: 'Any woman who bothers her husband and distresses him is distant from the blessings of Allah and any woman who respects her husband, is obedient and does not cause him sorrow, is blessed and prosperous.'"[35]

"There is a tradition reported that the Holy Prophet (S) was informed of a good woman who fasted everyday and worshipped Allah every night, but she had an ill-disposed character and would hurt her neighbours with her sharp tongue. 'The Holy Prophet (S) stated: 'There is no good in her and she is an inhabitant of hell.'"[36]

Wrong Expectations

Dear lady! You are the mistress of your household. Be wise and understanding. Keep an account of your expenses. Budget your

---

[33] Ibid, 3rd Shahriwar, 1349 Solar Hijri

[34] Bihar al-Anwar, vol 71, p 377

[35] Ibid, vol 103, p 253

[36] Ibid, vol 103, p 253

expenditures in a way that it is not detrimental to your wealth and honor. Do not compete with others and be envious of them. If you see a nice dress on a woman, or if you become interested in some furnishings that you have seen at a friend's or relative's house, do not compel your husband to purchase them which is beyond his nancial means and would force him to borrow. Isn't it better to wait until your budget is higher or there is some extra saving to make non-essential purchases?

It is mostly the ignorant and selsh women who succumb to extravagance and rivalry. These women force their husbands to be under debt and they become exhausted and disgusted in trying to satisfy the unsuitable demands of their wives. Sometimes, the only solution to these problems for the men is to go for a divorce or even commit suicide.

The women who have not perceived the true purpose and meaning of marriage and instead they regard it in terms of bondage where the husband is acquired to fulll their childish desires and material needs. They want a husband who will serve them like a slave and will not object to their way of spending. These women sometimes even go further. They make their husbands spend more than their means which may entail bankruptcy, murder, and other disastrous consequences.

Such women are a disgrace to other women. If her high expectations lead to divorce, the woman will be deprived of the love of her children, and will have to live a life of loneliness. For these women remarriage will not happen easily. Even if it does happen, it is not certain that the marriage will work out since most human beings do not like to be kept in unreasonable bondage and the new husband may not be able to meet their demands any better than the previous one.

Dear lady! Instead of being covetous, try to be reasonable. Spend more time and effort for the well- being of your family and husband rather than trying to imitate everyone. If your husband spends lavishly, then stop him and curb his unnecessary expenses. Instead of buying non-essential commodities, it is better to save some money for a rainy day.

"In a tradition, the Holy Prophet (S) stated: 'Any woman who is not compatible with her husband and persuades him to act beyond his capacity, then her deeds would not be accepted by Allah. She would taste the wrath of Allah on the Day of Resurrection.'"[37]

In another Tradition, the Holy Prophet (S) stated:

"Any woman who is not compatible with her husband, is not content with what Allah has blessed them with, and treats her husband harshly by demanding him to give more than he is able, then her acts (or worship) are not acceptable by Allah and He will be angry with her."[38]

"In other tradition, the Holy Prophet (S) stated: After having faith in Allah, there is not any greater blessing than to have a compatible spouse.'"[39]

Be a Comfort for Your Husband

The burdens of life weigh heavily upon the shoulders of men since they are responsible for maintaining and supporting their families. In fullling this responsibility, the man of the household must confront many problems and obstacles outside of the home. Some of these problems may be the pressures of work, the hassles of trafc and commuting from the ofce to home, concerns over economical and political issues of the day, empathy and concern for friends and colleagues, and the pressures of trying to improve the living conditions of his family. The amount of preoccupations and pressures upon a

---

[37] Bihar al-Anwar, vol 71, p 244

[38] Ibid, vol 76. p 367

[39] Mustadrak, vol 3, p 532

responsible man is enormous and multifaceted. It is no wonder that the average lifespan of a man is less than the woman.

In order for the human being to be able to cope with the burdens of life it is necessary to have someone to listen to and sympathize with him. Your husband is no exception. He may feel alone and in need of nding refuge and comfort amidst these pressures. It is natural that the man looks towards his wife and family as a source of comfort and relief. Therefore, anticipate his expectations and needs. Be cordial and warm when he rst returns home after working and have refreshments or let him feel that you are at his disposal to care for his needs. Try not to overwhelm him with criticizing him the minute you see him. Let him rest and recover his strength before putting up the demands of the family's personal issues.

When your husband comes home, try to have a smile and a warm greeting for him. Attend to his physical needs of fatigue, hunger, and thirst. Then ask him about his problems. If he is not willing to talk, be a good listener and sympathize with him. Try to express your genuine concern and then help him realize that the problems are not as impossible and huge as he had thought. Give him encouragements of support to help him cope with the issues. You can say something like this: These problems are being faced by many people. With a strong will-power and patience, it is possible to overcome the difculties as long as one does not let the problems get the better of you. These problems, as a matter of fact, are tests as well as builders of the true character of a person. Do not despair. You can solve them through determination and perseverance.

If you have some ideas on handling the problems, share them with your husband. If not, may be you can suggest a good friend who is more qualied.

Dear lady! at times of difculty, your husband is in need of your attention and love. You should come to his aid and nurse him like a sympathetic psychiatrist and wife. What a psychiatrist could give the amount of care that you would give? Do not underestimate your ability to soothe and strengthen him. There is no one more devoted and concerned over your husband's well-being other than yourself. He would be able to draw strength from your devotions to him and cope with his problems which will relieve his emotional and mental pressures. Consequently, the mutual bond of respect and love would also be greater which can only lead towards strengthening your marital relationship.

"In a tradition, Imam as-Sadiq (a.s) stated: 'There is nothing better in the world than a good wife. And a good wife is the one whose husband, becomes glad upon seeing her.'"[40]

"In a tradition, Imam Rida (a.s) stated: 'There are a group of women who raise many children. They are kind and sympathetic. They support their husbands in times of difculty and in the affairs of this world and the next. These women do not commit any acts which would incur a loss upon their husbands nor multiply their difculties.'"[41]

Be Appreciative

If a person is generous and charitable with the wealth that he has acquired from hard work, the appreciation and notice given in response to such acts will warm that person's inner feelings and give him a feeling of accomplishment. Acts of goodwill may then become second nature to the person whereby it becomes a habit to spend and share one's wealth for those in need. However, if the acts of goodwill are taken for granted and unappreciated, the person may lose the desire and drive to do good. It would be natural for a person to conclude that it was a

---

[40] Bihar al-Anwar, vol 103, p 217

[41] Mustadrak, vol 2, p 534

waste to give away his hard earned money when it was unappreciated.

Gratitude and appreciation are admirable characteristics in a person and it is the secret by which one may attract charitable acts. Even Allah has mentioned that gratitude for His blessings are conditional on the continual perpetuation of his grace upon mankind:

"And when your Lord made it known: If you are grateful would certainly give to you more, and if you are ungrateful, My chastisement is fully severe." (The Holy Qur'an, 14:7)

Dear Madam! Your husband is also human. Like everyone else, he enjoys being appreciated. He is willing to support his family and regards it as a moral and lawful obligation. When he is thanked and appreciated for doing his duty, those duties no longer seem to be a burden.

Whenever he buys home appliances or something like clothes and shoes for you and the children, be happy and thank him. Show your gratitude for the trivial things he does such as buying groceries, taking the family on trips and gives you your allowance. By showing your appreciation, you will make your husband feel good and rewarded for the trouble he has taken. Be careful that you do not take his duties for granted and become indifferent towards his contributions to the family. He may become disheartened about the welfare of the family. He may prefer to spend his money elsewhere or on himself.

If a friend or relative presented you with a pair of stockings or a bunch of owers, you would thank them repeatedly. So it is only natural and fair to show appreciation to your husband for his consideration and thoughtfulness. Do not think that you would be belittling yourself by demonstrating your appreciation. On the contrary, you would be loved and cared for more because you appreciate the efforts of your husband whereas snobbism and selshness can only lead towards great misfortunes.

The following are some Traditions referring to the characteristics of gratitude:

"Imam as-Sadiq (a.s) stated: 'The best women among your women are those who show appreciation when their husbands bring home something and are not discontented if nothing is brought home.'"[42]

"Imam as-Sadiq (a.s) also stated: ' Any woman who says to her husband that she has not seen any good things from him then she has fallen in her credibility and has voided her acts of worship.'"[43]

"The Messenger (SA) of Allah stated: 'Whoever does not thank the people who help him is, in fact, not showing his gratitude to Allah for His Blessings.'"[44]

Do not Look for Shortcomings

Nobody is perfect. Some are too tail or too short, or too fat or too skinny, have a big nose or a small one, talk too much or are too silent, are bad-tempered or too easy-going, have a very dark complexion or a very fair complexion, or eat too much, or too less, and the list can continue. Most men and women have some of these shortcomings. It is the hope of every man and woman to nd a spouse who is perfect but such hopes are unrealistic. It is unlikely to nd a woman who regards her husband as perfect.

Those women who are in search of faults in their husbands will undoubtedly nd them. They would nd a trivial shortcoming and exaggerate it by dealing on the matter to the point that it becomes an unbearable impediment. This defect then replaces all the merits of

---

[42] Bihar al-Anwar, vol 103, p 239

[43] Shafi, vol 2, p 139

[44] Wasa'il al Shiah, vol 11, p 542

the husband. They always compare their husbands with other men. They have established a so-called ideal man in their imaginations whose standards do not t in their husbands. Therefore, they are always complaining about the shortcomings in their marriage. The women regard themselves as unfortunates and failures which gradually turn them into spiteful women.

What does such behaviour in a woman do to her husband? He may be a very patient person who can tolerate his rudeness but most likely he will become insulted and develop a grudge against her. This would likely lead towards mutual arguments and elaborations of the shortcomings in each other. They will both become contemptuous of each other and their life wit! turn into a series of rows and arguments. Thus, they will either live in misery together or go for a divorce. In either case, both will lose, especially when there is no guarantee that another marriage may prove otherwise.

It is a pity that some women are ignorant and obstinate in their ignorance. It is possible that they may shatter their family life over a trivial matter. The following are some illustrative cases of such women:

"A woman left her husband and went to her father's house because her husband had bad breath. She was not prepared to go back home until he corrected his problem. On the basis of the husband's complaint, the court reconciled the couple and the wife returned to him. When the couple went home, the wife could still smell his bad breath so she went into another room. The husband went crazy and killed her.'"[45]

A female dentist divorced her husband because he was not on the same level as her; he had graduated three years after her.'"[46]

A woman applied for a divorce because her husband used to sit on the oor and eat with his ngers, did not shave everyday and did not

---

[45] Ittela'at, 7th Azar, 1350 Solar Hijri

[46] Ibid,17th Bahman, 1350 Solar Hijri

know how to socialize with others.'"[47]

Of course all women are not like this. There are those who are intelligent, realistic, and aware enough that they do not foolishly jeopardize their marriage and happiness by exaggerating the shortcomings of their husbands.

Dear Madam! Your husband is a human being like you. He is not perfect, but he may have many merits. If you are interested in your marriage and your family then do not set out to nd his weaknesses. Do not regard his small defects as important. Do not compare him with an ideal man whom you have established in your mind. There may be some faults with your husband which are not present in others. But you should remember that other men may have other defects which are non-existent in yours. Be satised with his merits. You will consequently see that his merits outweigh his faults. Besides why should you expect a perfect husband when you are imperfect yourself. If you are proud enough to think you are perfect, then ask others.

"The Prophet of Allah (S) stated: 'There is nothing worse for human beings than to seek the faults of others, while ignoring their own aws.'"[48]

Why should you exaggerate a trivial fault? Why should you shatter your life for the sake of something unimportant?

Be wise? Stop being frivolous! Ignore the faults and do not mention them in front of or behind your husband. Try to create a warm atmosphere in your family and enjoy the blessings of Allah. However, there may be aws in your husband's character which you may be able to correct. If so, then you can succeed only by behaving considerately and with patience. You must not criticize him or start a row, but approach him in a friendly manner.

---

[47] Ibid, 8th Esfand, 1350 Solar Hijri

[48] Bihar al-Anwar, vol 73, p 385

Don't Look at Anyone Other Than Your Husband

Dear lady! Before your marriage you may have had other offers of matrimony. These offers may be from rich, educated, handsome men, etc whom you may have wished to marry. Such expectations were natural before your marriage. But now that you have chosen your partner and signed a sacred covenant with him to be together for the rest of your life, then forget the past altogether. You must put aside your past wishes and forget those past offers. Do not think of any men except your husband and nd peace with him. If you do otherwise you will place yourself in a strained condition.

Now that you have agreed to live with your husband, why should you be constantly noticing other man? Why should you compare him with others? What do you achieve by looking at other men except putting yourself in a permanently miserable state and cause mental anguish for yourself?

"Imam Ali (a.s) stated: 'Whoever leaves his eyes at liberty, will always suffer through his nerves, and will be trapped in a permanent state of envy.'"[49]

By looking at other men and comparing your husband with them, you will nd a man who does not have your husband's faults. You might then think that man is perfect, because you are not aware of the deciencies of such a man. You regard your marriage as a failure and this thought might lead to disastrous ends.

"Mrs..., an 18-year old woman who had run away from home was arrested by the police last night. In the police station the woman said that, after three years of marriage, she gradually felt that she did not love her husband. She said: 'I'm used to compare my husband's face

---

[49] Bihar al-Anwar, vol 104, p 38

with other men and I regretted my marriage with him.'" [50]

Dear Madam! If you are interested in an everlasting marriage; if you do not want mental distress; and if you want to conduct a normal life, then stop being selsh and forget your vain hopes. Do not make compliments for other men. Do not think of any man other than your husband. Do not think to yourself:

"I wish I had married so and so;" "I wish my husband looked like...;" "I wish my husband's job was...;" "I wish...," "I wish..." "I wish..."

Why should you imprison yourself with these thoughts? Why should you upset the foundations of your marriage? If any of those wishes had come true, how would you know that you would have been more satised? Are you sure that the wives of those so-called "faultless" men are satised with them?

Dear Madam! If your husband suspects that you show interest in other men, he would be disheartened and would lose interest in you. You must not cut jokes with other men or keep company with them. Men are so sensitive that they cannot even tolerate their wives to show an interest in a picture of another man.

"The Holy Prophet (S) stated: 'Any married woman, who looks at other men, would be subject to the vehement wrath of Allah.'"[51]

Islamic Hijab

Men and women, although having many aspects in common, also possess unique characteristics. One such characteristic is that women are delicate, beautiful, and likable beings. They are charming, attractive, and lovable; whereas men are charmed, attracted by and love women's qualities.

---

[50] Ittela'at, 3rd Esfand, 1350 Solar Hijri

[51] Bihar al-Anwar, vol 104, p 39

When a man marries a woman, he wishes all his wife's beauty and affection to be reserved for him. He wishes to be the only one who benets from her charm, affection, coquettishness, beauty, sense of humour, etc and to strictly avoid men. Man is, by nature, very ardent and intolerant of another man either looking at his wife or having any kind of relationship with her. He would regard a close relationship between his wife and other men to be a violation of his lawful right. He expects his wife to observe Islamic Hijab (statutory Islamic dress for women) and by adapting herself to Islamic behaviour and ethics she cooperates in maintaining his lawful rights.

Any faithful and fervent man would have such a wish. A woman's social behaviour, which is based on Islamic ethics, would set her husband's mind at rest; he would then work enthusiastically to provide for his family and his affection for his wife would increase. Such a man would not be attracted to other women. On the contrary, a man whose wife is not concerned m with Islamic Hijab and displays her beauty to other men or socializes with them, would seriously become upset. He would regard his wife as responsible for trampling over his rights. Such a husband would always suffer from distress and pessimism and his love for his family may gradually fade away.

It is therefore in the interest of society and women that they should be dressed modestly and behave humbly; they should appear in public without any make-up and should abstain from showing off their beauty to others. Observing Hijab is an Islamic duty. The Almighty Allah says in the Holy Qur'an:

> ***"And say to the believing women that they should cast down their looks and guard their private parts, and not display their ornaments except what appears thereof, and let them wear their head coverings and not display their ornaments except to their husbands or their fathers. or the father of***

their husbands, their sons. or the sons of their husbands or their brothers or their brother's sons or their sisters' sons, or their women, or those whom their right hands possess, or male servants not having need (of women), or the children who have not attained knowledge of what is hidden of women; and let them not strike their feet so that what they hide of their ornaments may be known; and turn to Allah all of you, so that you may be successful." (The Holy Qur'an, 24:31).

Islamic Hijab and its observance in society is benecial to women in many aspects:

1. They can protect both their social worth and inner values much better, and guard themselves against just being an object on display.
2. They can prove both their faith and love for their husbands more effectively and thus help create and maintain a warm family atmosphere while preventing ill-feelings and family rows. In short, they can win their husband's hearts and establish themselves in their families.
3. By observing Islamic Hijab, unlawful irtation looks by such people as ogles would cease and help in lessening the amount of rows, strengthening the family roots, and as a result create an atmosphere of tranquility within its circle.
4. Islamic Hijab of women would also help prevent young unmarried men, from deviating from the right path. Thus forestalling harm to the young men, which would also benet the women of the society.
5. If all women observed the regulation of Islamic Hijab, then all women could rest assured that their husbands, when not at home

would not encounter a lewd woman who might draw his attention away from the family.

Islam is aware of woman's specic nature of creation and regards her as a very important base of society with responsibilities towards it. It demands her to make sacrices to carry out her responsibility by observing Islamic Hijab, which in turn would forestall social corruption and deviation and go a long way in creating stability, security and glorifying her nation. But denitely the greatest reward is with the Almighty Allah for performing her divine duty.

Dear lady! if you are interested in the stability and peace of your family and your husband's continual trust in you; if you are concerned about the social rights of women; if you are interested in the youth's mental health and are worried about their deviation from moral values, if you want to take positive steps towards bringing to a halt the seduction of women by corrupt men; and if you are seeking Allah's satisfaction by being a faithful and sacricing Muslim; then you should observe Islamic Hijab.

You should not display your beauty and adornments to strangers, be it in the house with your close relations or at other social gatherings outside your own home. You must cover yourself before your brothers-in-law and their sons, sister-in-law's husbands, aunts' husbands, and cousins. Being not dressed as per Islamic Hijab before these people is a sin and may also cause great distress to your husband, even though he may never mention it.

A woman is not restricted to covering herself to the same extent before her father-in-law, her own brother, and her nephews, although it is better to observe a certain degree of Islamic Hijab before these people too. In other words women should not appear before these relatives of hers in the same way as she would make herself attractive for her husband. This is because most men dislike their wives to appear attractive by wearing attractive clothes and make up before other men; and of course it should not be forgotten that the tranquility of mind and the trust of a man in his wife is crucial to the survival and security of the whole family.

Forgive Your Husband's Mistakes

Everyone, except those that Allah has declared as "Infallible" makes mistakes. When two people, who love together, and cooperate with each other, make mistakes, they must be forgiving, if they do not forgive each other, then their marriage will come to an end. Two business partners, two neighbours, two colleagues, two friends, and specically, a husband and a wife need to be able to forgive each other. If the members of a family are unforgiving and pursue each other's mistakes, then either the family will separate or they will experience an unbearable life.

Dear Madam! Your husband probably makes mistakes. He may insult you, abuse you, tell lies, he might even hit you. Such acts might be committed by any man. If your husband, after making a mistake, regrets it or you feel he is regretful himself for his misconduct, then forgive him and do not pursue the matter. If he is regretful but not prepared to express his apologies, then do not try to prove his mistake. Otherwise, he might feel humiliated and he may retaliate by picking out your mistakes and consequently start a major row. So it is better for you to remain silent until he condemns himself from his conscience and starts to feel remorse about it. He would then regard you as wise and devoted wife who is interested in her husband and family.

"The Prophet of Allah (S) stated: 'A bad woman does not forgive her husband's mistake and does not accept his apology.'"[52]

Is it not pitiful that a sacred marital covenant should be broken

---

[52] Bihar al-Anwar, vol 103, p 235.

because a woman is not prepared to forgive some mistakes of her husband?

Coping with Your Husband's Relatives

One of the problems of family life is the one cause between the wife and her husband's relatives. Some women do not have a good relationship with their husband's mother, sisters, or brothers. On the one hand the wife may try to dominate her husband so that he would not be able to pay any attention even to his mother, or any other relatives and she may try to sow discord between them.

On the other hand, her mother-in-law regards herself as the owner of her son and daughter-in-law. The mother tries hard to hold on to her son and is watchful that the new woman does not try to possess him fully. She may fabricate lies about her daughter-in-law or nd fault in her. Such an attitude might be followed by many arguments and even occasional hostilities. The situation becomes even worse if they all live in the same house. Even though a row may occur between two women, the real anguish and distress remains with the man in the middle.

The husband is trapped in an argument where he cannot take sides. On the one hand is his wife who would like to have an independent life without any interference from outsiders. He naturally feels that he must support her and make her happy. But on the other hand, he thinks of his parents who have helped him with his life, education, and have spent their own lives in bringing him up. He feels that his parents expect him to help them in their times of need and that it would not be fair to abandon them.

Besides, if he himself was in need of something, who else, other than his parents, would help him and his family. As a result, he realizes that his best and most trustworthy friends are his parents and relatives.

So, the dilemma for a sensible man is either to choose the wife and abandon the parents or vice versa; but neither of these is possible.

Consequently, he has to cope with both sides and keep them satised which, itself, is a difcult task. The only possible way to ease the situation is that the woman should be loyal and wise. A man in this situation expects his wife to help solve the problem. If the wife respects her mother-in-law, seeks advice from her, and becomes obedient and friendly with her, then the mother-in-law will be her greatest supporter.

Is it not sad that one, who can attract many people through kindness and good manners, should repulse them through stubbornness and selshness? Do you not realize that in the ups and downs of life, one might need the help of others, and especially of relatives who would support you when everyone else deserts you? Is it not better to enjoy a good relationship with one's relatives through consideration and good behaviour? Is it really wise and fair to become friends with strangers while breaking away from your own relations?

Experience shows that when one needs the help of others, friends leave but the abandoned relatives come to help. This is because the family ties are natural and cannot be broken easily. There is a general proverb which says: "Even if one's esh is eaten by relations, they would not throw away the bones!"

"Imam Ali (a.s) stated: 'One is never able to do without his relatives, even though he may possess wealth and children.'"[53]

One would need the respect and kindness of one's relatives. It is they who would support one physically and mentally. Relatives always come to the rescue. In times of need they could come to one's assistance faster than others. Whoever disowns his relatives will lose many helping hands.

---

[53] Bihar al-Anwar, vol 74, p 101

Dear Madam! For the sake of your husband and for the sake of your own comfort as well as to nd many good friends and supporters, put up with your husband's relatives. Do not be selsh and ignorant; be wise and do not cause your husband any distress. Be a good and devoted wife in order to be accepted by both Allah and the people.

Coping With Your Husband's Job

Everyone has a job and jobs are different. For example, a driver who is mostly on the road and is unable to come home every night; a policeman who may have to stay out some nights; a medical doctor who has little time to spend with his family; a lecturer or a scientist who reads a great deal at nights; a mechanic whose clothes are dirty and have smell of oil; a factory worker who works at night. Therefore, there are rarely jobs which are entirely convenient and do not entail any discomfort of the family. There is not any other way of earning an honest living than working. It is necessary for the men to put up with the difculties of their jobs. However, there is another problem which is the complaints of the family.

Women usually like their men to be nearby and prefer them to be home when it becomes dark. Women want their husbands to have a decent job with a high salary. They like to have enough time to go out in the evenings. But unfortunately, the jobs of most men do not live up to their wives' expectations, and this, for some families, is a source of rows and arguments.

A driver who has been on the road for a few nights, who has not had a decent sleep and has not been eating regularly, enters his house to rest and nd peace and comfort with his family. Then his wife, without sparing a moment, starts to moan and groan: "What is this life? Why do you leave me with these kids and where have you been? I have to do all the work myself because you are not here to help. I am fed up with these naughty children. As a matter of fact driving is not a good job. You should either change your job or settle with me. I can't live like this any longer!"

A poor driver who has such a wife cannot be expected to perform well on his job and may endanger his life; and the lives of those whom he transports. A doctor who, from morning to night, visits tens of patients cannot cope with the grumbling of his wife. Then how could he continue to practise medicine? A worker who works during the night shifts cannot enthusiastically pursue his job if his wife is a shrewish woman. How can a scientist be successful in his eld of research if his wife is constantly nagging him? These are the tests which distinguish the wise women from the ignorant ones.

Dear Madam! We cannot make the world according to our wishes, but we can adapt ourselves to the existing situation. Your husband needs to have a job to earn his family's living. His job has certain conditions which you must adapt to. You must program your family life according to his job. Why do you grumble and nd fault with his job? Welcome him home with a happy face and be kind to him. Be wise and cope with his job.

If your husband is a driver who is mostly on the road, then realize that he is trying to bring money home for your sake and the children's. There is nothing wrong with his job. He is a part of society and is serving it the best way he can. Would it have been better if he was a lazy person or if he was engaged in an irreligious job? So, there is nothing wrong with him. The fault lies with you, expecting him to be at home every night and not being able or not wanting to adapt yourself to the present conditions.

Is it not wise to get used to the existing situation and live more comfortably? Would you not rather welcome him with a smiling face and persuade him to carry on in his job with a warm "Good-bye" when he leaves home for work? If you act kindly, his interest in his family would increase and he could work harder. He would not isolate himself from you; he would come home as early as possible; he would not have accidents and he would remain healthy in his morals.

If your husband is a night-shift worker, he is missing his night's good sleep in order to meet the expenses of his family. Try to get used to it and do not express your dissatisfaction. If you get bored, then you can do some of the housework, sewing and reading at night. In the morning prepare the breakfast when your husband comes back from work, and then prepare his bed in a quiet place. Keep the children quiet and teach them not to disturb their father when he is resting. You can even sleep less at night and take a rest with your husband during the day. But, do not forget that he has been awake all the night and the sleep during the day to him is the same as the night sleep for you. Women in this situation have to have two programs, one for themselves and one for their husbands.

If your husband is a driver, a doctor, a worker, or a scientist etc, then you must be proud of him. Your husband is not an idle loafer or engaged in an irreligious occupation. So appreciate him and show your gratitude.

Do not expect him or ask him to leave his job, but try to adapt to his existing one. If he is reading or researching on a particular eld, then do not disturb him. You can do the housework, read a book or, with his permission, go and visit your friends or relatives. But when he is resting, try to be at home. Prepare his food and other requirements. Receive your husband with a smiling face and good manners. By showing your kindness and by pleasing him you can make him forget his tiredness. If you are a good wife, then not only you can expedite his promotion, but also you are contributing to his services towards society.

Not all women deserve such hardworking men. So by being well-mannered and sacricing, prove that you are worthy of him.

If your husband's job requires him to wear special clothes which become dirty, then wash them frequently. Do not grumble and do not tell him bad because of his job. Do not ask him to change his job. It is not easy to change jobs. What is wrong with being a mechanic? In any case, this is not an important matter and families should not be broken because of it.

"A woman told the judge in a court that her husband's job was selling kerosene and that he always smelled bad and hence she was fed up with the situation."[54]

If You Have to Live Away From Your Hometown

One may have to live away from one's hometown. Your husband may be working for the private or the public sector and sent on duty to another city or town also. Some people live in this way either temporarily or permanently. Men are forced to cope with this situation but some women prefer to be near their parents and relatives. These women are accustomed to the streets, walls, and the environment of their place of birth. After moving away they blame their husbands and complain: "Why should I live away from my home? How long am I going to be away from my home and my parents? I have no one in this place. What is this place you have brought me? I cannot stay here; so think of a way out!"

These women should not upset their husbands in this way. They are so feeble-minded that they think their birth places are the best locations to live. They think that they cannot enjoy life anywhere else.

Mankind is not satised even with its own planet, so it has stepped onto other planets. But one looks and nds a woman who is so improvident that she is not prepared to live a few miles away from her

---

[54] Ittela'at, 13 Murdad, 1349 Solar Hijri

hometown. She thinks to herself: "Why should I leave all my friends and relatives to get to a strange place?' It is as if this lady is not self-condent enough to be able to nd new friends in another place away from her home.

Dear Madam! Be wise and sacricing. Do not be selsh. Now that your husband's job has taken you away from your hometown, do not cause him any distress. If he is a civil servant, he has orders to travel on duty and if he has a private business, then surely it is to his advantage to live in another location. If your husband informs you that he has to live in another place, then you should agree at once. You should then help pack up and move to new places where you must try to feel at home. Plan your life in this new home and adapt yourself to it. Since you are new in the area and probably not familiar with the characteristics of the inhabitants, be cautious with them. After a while, with the help and supervision of your husband, try to make friends from among the chaste and trustworthy women.

Every place has its own merits. You can relax by sightseeing and visiting ancient buildings. You must keep the family together and encourage your husband in his work. After a while you get used to your new home and you might even like it more than your previous one. You might nd that your new friends are better than your old ones.

If the new place lacks the luxury of your previous town, then get used to the new life and nd its merits. If you are no longer enjoying such privileges as electricity, then your environment may have a better climate and you may be able to get fresher and better quality food. If there are not any proper roads, then you will not be inhaling toxic exhaust fumes and you will be away from all the noise of people and cars.

Think a little about your country men and women who are living happily in mud and brick houses and would not give any heed to the luxuries of city life and their beautiful castle-like houses. Think of their needs and deprivations. If you can help them, then do not hesitate and encourage your husband to be helpful to them. If you are wise and perform your duty, then you can live comfortably in the new place. You can be helpful towards your husband's progress. This way you would be known as a respected and devoted wife. You will be loved by your husband and would earn popularity amongst the people.

Moreover Allah will be satised with you.

If Your Husband Works at Home

Those women whose husbands work outside have freedom at home. But some men work at home, like poets, writers, painters, or scientists who need to read a great deal. The wives of such men have less freedom at home and, therefore their lives are different. The above-mentioned jobs require concentration, talent, and intellect. Therefore, there will be a need for privacy and silence. One hour of work in peace is equivalent to a few hours of work in a busy and noisy surrounding. The problem is clear. On the one hand, the man needs a quiet place to work in and on the other hand, the wife wants to move around the house freely.

If a woman plans the affairs of such a house in such a way that her husband can get on with his job, surely she has accomplished a valuable task. Such an achievement is certainly not easy, especially when there are children around. But nevertheless the problem must be solved, because the progress of the husband in his job would be based on this.

If a woman cooperates with her husband, she can turn him into a respected man who can be a credit to her and the society.

A woman, whose husband works at home, should not expect him to baby sit, to open the door to callers, to go to the kitchen, to help with the housework, to shout at the children...; but she should imagine that he is not in the house while he is working.

Dear Madam! When your husband wants to go to his study room, prepare his pen, paper, cigarettes, ash-tray, matches, books, and other items he requires.

Once you have prepared the room and his requirements, leave him. Do not talk loudly and do not allow the children to make a noise. Teach your children not to play noisily while their father is working. Do not talk to him about daily matters. Answer the door and the telephone when it rings. If anybody wants to see him or talk to him, tell them he is busy. Entertain your guests during his break times. Tell your friends and relatives to visit you when your husband is not busy. Your true friends would not be upset by your demand. While you are doing your housework, provide him with his needs. Do not interrupt him.

Perhaps some women think this way of life is impossible. They might say: "Is it possible for a woman to do the difcult housework, and at the same time, take care of her husband and not to let anything interrupt him?"

It is true that this way of life is unusual and seems difcult, but if the women in question ponder over the importance of their husbands' jobs, they can decide to overcome the problem through good planning, devotion, and wisdom. The exceptionality of some women becomes apparent in these situations.

Otherwise, running an ordinary family life is not an extraordinary task.

Dear lady! Writing a book, a good scientic article or a useful essay, writing an excellent poem, creating a precious painting, or solving scientic problems are not easy tasks. But, with your devotion and co-operation it becomes possible. Are you not prepared to sacrice your desires and with a slight alteration in your life, help your husband in his job? Through your help, he would become prestigious and you would share his social status.

Help Your Husband to Make Progress

Human beings are by nature potentially able to make progress. The love for attaining perfection exists in all of us; and we have been created for achieving perfection. Everyone, in any job at any age and in any condition is able to progress and mature. One should never be content with mere existence, and should not forget the purpose of creation. One must try to acquire perfection in one's own lifetime.

Even though everyone is pursuing for progress, not all are successful. Making progress needs high aspirations and a great deal of hard work. One must prepare the ground and remove the obstacles after which one must take the necessary steps in the path of progress. The personality of a man is largely dependent on his wife's desires. A woman can be helpful in her husband's progress as much as she could be detrimental to it.

Dear lady! While considering the possibilities, consider a higher status for your husband and encourage him to achieve it. If he is interested in continuing his studies or if he wants to increase his knowledge through reading and research, then do not stop him. Encourage him to achieve his desires. Plan your life in a way that is not a hindrance in his progress. Try to assist him to make progress through creating a relaxed and comfortable atmosphere at home. If he is illiterate, encourage him and humbly ask him to start his studies at night classes. If he is educated, encourage him to increase his knowledge by further reading. If he is a medical doctor, make him read the medical journals and other related articles. If he is a teacher, engineer or a judge, then ask him to read the books and articles which are related to his specialization. You should remember whatever position your husband holds, there is an opportunity for him to make progress.

Do not let him deviate from the path which has been paved by the order to creation. Encourage him to read books. Do not let his personality cease to grow.

If he is short of time to buy or obtain books, then with his or a friend's supervision obtain the books of his
interest. Give the books to him and encourage him to read them. You should read books and useful magazines too. If through reading, you come across an article which is useful for your husband, then inform him of it. This act has several benets:

1. Through the repetition of this act, your husband will become a learned person who would be a credit to you and himself. Moreover, he would become a brilliant specialist whose services would be benecial to him as well as his society.
2. Since, through his studies and research, he has conformed with the laws of creation, he would be less prone to mental and nervous disorders.
3. Since he is on the path to progress and shows interest in reading, then he becomes more attached to you and the children; he would not be drawn towards corrupt activities and would not fall into the trap of fatal addictions.

Be Careful That He is Not Misled

Men should have freedom in their business and associations in order to be able to work and progress in a way suitable to them. If men are restricted in their activities, then they will not be comfortable. A wise woman would not interfere with the affairs of her husband. She should not monitor his movements; because she should know that by denying him the freedom he needs and by trying to control his activities, he may react severely.

Wise and experienced men do not need to be controlled. Such men always act wisely; they cannot be deceived; they know both their friends and their foes. However, there are men who are simple; they can easily be deceived and would easily be inuenced by others.

There are people who are impostors and are lying in wait for simple men. The impostor, though pretending to be a good-doer, traps the man and draws him towards corruption. The corrupt society and the unyielding nature of humans does not help the situation. The simple man may not realize his situation for a while, but one day he wakes up and nds himself deep in a trap from which there is not any escape.

If you look around yourself, you see tens of such unfortunate people. Perhaps none of them intended to fall in the trap or become corrupt, but through their own simplicity, ignorance, and unthoughtfulness, they are now preyed upon by the corrupt in society.

On this account, the simple men need to be taken care of. By monitoring their activities, the wise and well-wishing people would be doing them a great service.

The best people for this task, however, are the wives of these men. A wise and clever wife is able, through a benevolent and wise attitude, to achieve the greatest of the tasks regarding her husband.

Such women, however, should remember not to directly interfere with the affairs of their husband, or to tell them the "do's" and the "don'ts". The reason for this is because men mostly do not like to be treated as tool in the hands of others; otherwise they may react sharply. But a wise woman would monitor her husband's activities and watch his associates indirectly without his knowledge.

It also happens that some men, some times, come back home later than usual. If this is the case and the number of the late arrivals to home are within an acceptable limit, then there is no need to worry, because men are sometimes engaged in certain unexpected events which they try to pursue after their work. However, if the number of late arrivals exceeds the accepted limit, then his wife should make an effort to investigate. But investigation is not easy; it requires patience and wisdom; one must avoid anger or protest.

The wife should rst of all talk to him softly and kindly. She should ask him why he came home later than the day before and where he had been. She should pursue the matter wisely and patiently at different times and on different occasions. If she nds out that he comes back home late because of his work or attends scientic, religious, and moral meetings, then she should leave him alone. If she feels that he has found a new friend, she should nd out who he is. If his new friend is a well-mannered person with a clean record, then she should not worry. It is even recommended that she encourages him in his new friendship, because a good friend is a great blessing.

If you feel that your husband is going astray or that he associated with corrupt and unworthy people, then you should stop him immediately. A woman in this situation has a great responsibility. The slightest mishandling of the situation, through carelessness. May shatter their family life. This is a situation where the wisdom and cleverness of some women can become useful and apparent. One should remember that rows or arguments are not the solution and they may result in the exact opposite. A woman, who experiences this event, has two tasks to achieve:

1. First she should assess the situation at home; and should examine herself and her attitude. She must nd out the reason for her husband's behavior. She should fairly judge why he has grown cold towards his family and gone astray. She may nd that her own attitude had been the cause; or perhaps she had been the cause; or perhaps she had been indifferent to his desires for food, her looks or the affairs of the house. Such matters draw men away from home. They may then pursue outside deviant activities in order to forget their problems. The wife can ask her husband about his

problems and try to help solve them. If a woman corrected herself and changed the house according to his desires, then she could be hopeful that her husband could be drawn back to his family and that he would avoid corrupt places.

2. Secondly, she should show him as much kindness as possible. She should advise him and remind him of the grim consequences of his deeds. She should even cry and beg him to give up his bad companions. She must say to him:

"I love you from the bottom of my heart. I am proud of you. I prefer you to all things and I am ready to devote myself to you. But I am saddened by one thing; why should a man, like you, have these kinds of friends; or attend that kind of a party? Such deeds are not suitable for you. Please give them up"

The wife must continue this attitude until she conquers the heart of her husband.

It is possible that the husband is used to unworthy habits and that he would not be inuenced easily, but the wife should not become disappointed. She should pursue her goal with greater strength and patience.

Women have great power and inuence over men. She is able to do whatever she wills if she puts her mind to it. If a woman decides to save her husband from the lth of corruption, she can do it. There is an eighty per cent chance of success, provided she acts wisely. Anyway, she must not use violence or a harsh attitude, unless she sees that there is not any result from being kind and gentle to him. Even then she must quarrel, leave home or use any other way in as kind a way as possible and not revengefully.

Yes, looking after one's husband is the duty of every wife. It is a difcult duty and that is why the Prophet of Islam stated: "The Jihad of a woman is to take care of her husband well."⁵⁵

Suspicious Women

It is not wrong if a woman is watchful of her husband, but only if it does not exceed to a state of suspicion and mistrust. Suspicion is a destructive and incurable illness. Unfortunately some women are affected by this disease.

A woman of suspicion imagines that her husband is, lawfully or unlawfully, disloyal to her. She imagines that he is married to another woman or that he is going to marry her. She suspects him of having an affair with his secretary or another woman. She loses trust in him because he comes home late or he was seen talking to a woman. If he helps a widow and her children, the wife may think that he has an interest in her, other than a charitable one. If any woman gives her husband a compliment, saying that he is handsome or well-mannered, she concludes that he is interested in that woman. Upon nding a strand of hair in his car, she thinks there is another woman in his life.

Such women with these thoughts and inconclusive proof gradually assume certainty regarding their husbands' unfaithfulness.

They think about it every day and night. They also tell others, friends and foes about it, who, in the name of sympathy, reinforce the allegations and in turn tell the concerned women about other unfaithful men.

Arguments and rows start to take shape. The woman begins to ignore the affairs of the house and the children and might even go to her parents. She would monitor him and search his pockets. She would read his letters and would explain any trivial matter as due to his unfaithfulness.

---

[55] Bihar al-Anwar, vol 103, p 247

With this attitude, she would make the family's life hard and turn the house into a burning hell in which she would also suffer. If her husband brought proof of his innocence, or swore that he had not been committing any thing wrong, or cried, she would not be satised.

The reader has certainly come across such women, but it is useful to know of the following cases:

"A woman said in the family court: 'Do not be surprised as to why, after twelve years of married life and three small children, I have decided upon a separation from my husband. I am now certain that my husband is unfaithful to me. A few days ago, I saw him with an attractive woman walking in the street. I read a weekly magazine which has a proper section on fortune telling. Every week, in my husband's horoscope, it mentions that he would have good times with the people who are born in the month of June. I was born in February; so I am not one of those people mentioned in the horoscope. Besides I feel my husband is not as loving towards me as he used to be'.

The husband of this woman said: "Please tell me what I can do I wish these magazines would consider the readers like my wife, and would not tell so many lies. Believe me these horoscopes have turned the lives of mine and my children into ruins. If one of these horoscopes says that this week a large lump sum of money is coming my way, then she comes to me and asks me what I have done with that money? Or, if it says that I would be receiving a letter, then Allah save me! I think it is probably better for both of us to separate, because she does not confront reason.'"[56]

"A man said in the court: 'It was a month ago, when I was coming back from a party, that of my colleagues asked me to give him and his wife a lift back home. The day after my wife asked me to take her to her parents'. On the way, she looked back and found a strand of hair on

---

[56] Ittela'at, 4th Dey, 1350 Solar Hijri.

the back seat of the car. She asked who this strand of hair belonged to. I was in a panic and could not give her a proper explanation. I dropped her at her parents' house and went to work. When I went to pick her up that night she refused to come with me. I asked, why? She said to me that I should better live with the owner of the strand of hair.'"[57]

"A young woman complained to the court and said: 'My husband is coming home late every night on account of overtime at his work. I have been worried about this and my suspicion has increased due to what our neighbours are saying. They say that my husband is lying and he is not working at night and that he goes after his pleasure. As a result I am not prepared to live with a liar'.

At his point the husband took out a few letters from his pocket and placed them on a counter before the judge and asked him to read them aloud in order to prove his innocence and to stop his wife's improper attitude.

The judge started to read the letters aloud. One of the letters was indicative of his overtime working from 4 to 8 O'clock at night. Other letters were also related to his work where he was asked to attend certain seminars. The wife came forward and after seeing the letters said: 'I used to search his pockets every night but I did not see any of these letters'..

The judge said: 'He might have left them at his work'.

The young man said: 'My wife's suspiciousness towards me has grown so much that I have become suspicious of her. Every night I have nightmares. I imagine that she is in love with a man and wants to separate from me in order to marry him'.

At this point the young wife rushed towards her husband and while crying for joy, apologized to him and they both left the court.'"[58]

---

[57] Ibid, 7th Dey, 1350 Solar Hijri

[58] Ibid, 29th Dey, 1348 Solar Hijri

"A dentist complained to the court and said: 'My wife is exceedingly jealous. I am a dentist and there are women patients who come to my ofce for treatment. This has aroused my wife's jealousy and everyday we argue about it. She believes that I should not accept women patients. But I cannot lose my regular patients. I love my wife and she loves me, but this improper expectation of hers is ruining our lives. A few days ago she came to my dental surgery and forced me to leave. We went home and quarreled.

She said to me: 'I went to your surgery and sat beside a young girl in the waiting room. We talked about you and she, without knowing that I was your wife, said: 'The dentist is a handsome and well- mannered man' . "The dentist went on saying: 'On account of a girl's opinion, my wife dragged me out of the surgery in a degrading manner.'"[59]

"A woman, complaining to the court, said: 'One of my friends told me that my husband goes to a stranger woman's house. I followed him one day and realized that it was true. Now I am asking the court to punish him'. The husband, while acknowledging what his wife was saying, told the court: 'One day I went to a pharmacy to buy some medicine. I saw a woman in the pharmacy who was buying powdered milk. She did not have enough money to pay for the milk, so I offered to help. Later, I found out that she was a widow who was poor. So I decided to continue my help.'" The judges, after investigating the matter, realized the truth of his claims and reconciled the couple.'"[60]

Such events happen in many families. The family atmosphere changes into an environment of pessimism, suspicion, and enmity. The children would suffer and the mental effects are grave.

If a couple continues to live in this situation, then they would both suffer, and if they show stubbornness towards each other, they would

---

[59] Ibid, 17th Tir, 1349 Solar Hijri

[60] Ibid, 25th Tir, 1349 Solar Hijri

surely lead to a divorce. In the case of a divorce taking place, both man and wife would be losers, because on the one hand the man would not be able to nd another wife who is any better than the previous one. On the other hand, the children would suffer and would not be able to enjoy a healthy life. The children might even confront new problems due to a step-father or step-mother.

The man may think that by divorcing his wife, he can marry a 'perfect' woman, with whom he can live in peace. But this is nothing more than a dream and the realization of it is very remote. By divorcing his wife, he may encounter new problems with the new one.

Divorce is also not a path to comfort and happiness for the woman. Although she might feel satised that she has had her revenge, remarrying would not be easy for her. She may have to live alone for the rest of her life and would probably not even enjoy the presence of her children. Even if she gets married again, it is not certain that her new husband would comply with her expectations. She may even have to bring up the children of a man whose wife is dead. Therefore, neither divorce nor arguments and rows can save the couple. But there is a way to salvation.

The best attitude is that both man and wife give up arguing and try to be logical. Men have a greater responsibility in this matter, and in fact the key to the solution is in their hands. Men can, through patience and forgiveness, save themselves from trouble and also help eliminate the element of suspicion in their wives.

Now a few words to the men:

Firstly, dear sir! You should remember that your wife, even though suspicious of you, loves you. She is interested in your children and the family home. She is afraid of separation. She would denitely suffer from your deplorable life situation. If she did not love you, she would not have been jealous. So she does not like the present situation, but what can she do if she is ill? Some patients have rheumatism and some have cancer. Your wife suffers from a mental disorder and if you do not believe it, then take her to a psychiatrist. You should treat her sympathetically and compassionately. You should not be angry with her or have arguments. No one could quarrel with an ill person. Do not react harshly to her impoliteness or allegations. Do not end up ghting with her. Do not go to any courts. Do not ignore her. Do not talk about divorce and separation. None of these acts can cure her illness; in fact it might become worse.

Your unkindness would serve as a source of her suspicion.

You must be as kind to her as possible. You might resent your wife deeply because of her attitude, but there is not any other way. You must treat her in a manner so that she becomes certain of your innocence.

Secondly, you should try to create an understanding between yourselves. Do not hide any thing from her. Let her read your letters even before you do. Leave the keys to your private desk, drawers or safe within her reach. Let her look into your bags and pockets. Allow her to monitor you. You should not express displeasure with any of the above- mentioned points, but regard them as normal procedures in a healthy and friendly family life.

After work, if you do not have any other business, return home as soon as possible. If an urgent matter arises that you should attend to, then inform your wife and tell her where you are going and at what time she should expect you back home. Then try to be on time. If you are late in coming home, then immediately tell your wife the reason. Be careful not to lie, otherwise she will become suspicious.

Consult her in your affairs. Do not hide anything from her. Talk to her about your day. Keep her trust in you. Ask her to question you on any vague subject which may be bothering her.

Thirdly, you may be innocent of the subject of her suspicion, but the suspicions of women are mostly not baseless either. Perhaps, through carelessness you have done something which has affected her mentally and made her suspicious of you. You should ponder over your previous acts carefully. You might then nd the cause of her suspicion. In this way you can solve the problem better. For instance, if you joke a lot with other women, try not to do it any more.

What is the point of being called handsome or well-mannered at the expense of your wife's suspicion and her distrust towards you? Why should you trigger her suspicion by joking with your secretary or a woman colleague? Why should you employ a woman to work for you? Do not joke with other women in parties. If you want to help a poor widow, why should you not inform your wife? You can even help the widow through your wife. Do not think that you are a slave, or a person in chains. You should not be a slave, but a wise man who, upon an agreement with your wife, is taking care of her. You should help her overcome this problem.

Through patience and wisdom, you should remove the dangers which are threatening the foundation of your sacred family life. You would then cure your wife's illness as well as save your children from unhappiness. You would do a great deal of service to yourself both mentally and materialistically.

Moreover, Allah rewards men who are willing to sacrice at vital moments such as this.

"Imam Ali (a.s) stated: ' Act moderately with the women in every instance. Speak to them nicely in order that their deeds become good.'"[61]

"Imam Sajjad (a.s) stated: 'One of the rights of a woman upon her husband is that he should forgive her ignorance and foolishness.'"[62]

"The Prophet of Allah (S) stated: ' Any man who copes with his incompetent wife, the Almighty Allah, upon his patience (towards his

---

[61] Bihar al-Anwar, vol 103, p 123

[62] Ibid, vol 74, p 5

wife) on every occasion, would grant him the reward of patience of Hadrat Ayyub (a.s).'"⁶³

Now the women are reminded of few points:

First:

Dear Madam! The subject of your husband's unfaithfulness, like every other subject, needs proof. As long as his guilt is not proved you do not have any right to convict him. Neither law nor one's conscience allows one to accuse someone on the account of probability of a crime having taken place. Would you not be hurt if someone accused you of something without any proof? Is it possible to consider your foolish and baseless theories as proof of an important crime such as adultery?

> *"O you who believe! avoid most of suspicion, for surely suspicion in some cases is a sin..." (The Holy Qur'an, 49:12)*

"Imam as-Sadiq (a.s.) stated: '(The weight of) accusing an innocent person falsely is heavier than the high mountains.'"⁶⁴

"The Prophet of Allah (S) stated: " Anyone who makes false accusations upon a believer, Allah, on the Day of Resurrection, will place him upon a heap of re in order that he receives the punishment he deserves.'"⁶⁵

Dear Madam! Do not be foolish and do not jump to conclusions. When you have time, sit down and write down all the proof and grounds regarding your husband's unfaithfulness. Then in front of each point, write down the other aspects to the problem and the probability of their occurrence. Next, place yourself as a fair judge and think deeply

---

⁶³ Ibid, vol 76, p 367

⁶⁴ Ibid, vol 75, p 194

⁶⁵ Ibid

about the written points. If they do not convince you that he is guilty, then you can either forget the matter or make further investigations.

For instance, the presence of a strand of hair in your husband's car may be easily explained by one of the following:

1. It may belong to one your husband's relatives such as his sister, mother, aunt, or their children.
2. It may be one of your own.
3. He might have given a lift to his friend or relative accompanying his wife and the strand of hair might be hers.
4. He might have given a lift to a helpless woman.
5. Perhaps one of his enemies has dropped the strand of hair in his car deliberately in order to make you suspicious of him.
6. One of his women colleagues might have been given a lift in his car.
7. There is also a probability that he had been out with his beloved. But this case is far more remote than the previous ones and therefore should not be taken very seriously. At least one should not regard it as rm evidence of guilt while forgetting about the other possibilities.

If your husband comes back home late, he might have been doing extra work; or might have been at his friend's house; or might have attended a seminar or a religious meeting; or he might even have walked back home.

If a woman thinks of him as a handsome man, it is not his fault. Being well-behaved is not a proof of being guilty! Would you prefer him to be a bad-tempered man from whom everyone would be repulsed?

If your husband attends to the needs of a widow and her children, regard him as a charitable person who is doing this for the sake of Allah.

If your husband has a private desk or a safe; and if he does not let you read his letters, do not think of him as having a mistress. Men generally have a sense of secrecy and modesty. They do not like others to be informed of their affairs, perhaps they possess secret materials which are related to their work.

Perhaps he does not regard you as a person who could keep a secret. Any way, a possibility is just that, and it should not be considered as a rm proof.

Second:

Whenever you suspect anything, you should discuss it with your husband in such a manner as to nd the truth of the matter out and not in a way of protest. Be frank with him and ask him to explain the subject of your suspicion in order to clear your mind and set it at peace. Then listen to him carefully. Think about his explanation. If you are satised with it then the matter is over. But if you are still suspicious, then investigate the matter yourself until the truth is revealed.

If, while investigating, you come across a point that your husband had lied about, then do not regard it as a proof of his guilt. This is because despite his innocence, he might have deliberately not been telling the whole truth lest you become more suspicious. Again it is better to go to him and ask why he did not tell the whole truth. Of course, it is not good for one to lie, but if your husband made this mistake, then you should not, in turn, act foolishly.

Ask him rmly to tell you the truth. His inability in explaining the subject of your suspicion is not indicative of his guilt. It is possible that he may really forget something or he may be in a panic. At this point, do not pursue the matter further and leave it for a more appropriate occasion. If he says to you that he has forgotten something, accept it. However, if you are still in doubt, investigate through other channels.

Third:

Do not voice your suspicion with anyone you see, since they may be your foes. Enemies always endorse your claims and might even add a few lies to it in order to shatter your life. They may not be foes, but a bunch of foolish, simple, and inexperienced people who reinforce your claims sympathetically. They may be you r close relatives or close friends. Consultation is only useful with wise, clever, and genuine sympathizers. If you need to consult someone, then nd the right people and discuss it with them.

Fourth:

If the proof of your husband's guilt is not a rm proof towards your husband's guilt, if your friends and relatives think that the evidence is not enough, if your husband regards himself as not guilty, and nally if you are still suspicious of him, then you can be sure that you are ill. You are suffering from a mental disorder in which the element of suspicion has grown beyond your control. It is vital for you to turn to a psychiatrist who could treat you accordingly.

Fifth:

Therefore, it is not wise for you to argue with you r husband or make complaints to the court. Do not talk about divorce and do not degrade him. Such an attitude will only lead to more anger and rows which may result in divorce. Be careful not to act foolishly, or decide to commit suicide. By killing yourself not only would you lose this life, but you would also be tormented in the next world. Is it not sad to lose your life for the sake of a baseless thought? Is it not better to solve your problems through patience and wisdom?

Sixth:

If you are still suspicious of your husband or you reach the conclusion that he is certainly having an affair, then again you are to be blamed, because you have not tried enough to win his heart. You have placed a gap in his life in which other woman can nd a place. But do not despair; there is still time.

Review your attitude and act in a manner that would attract your husband towards you.

Do Not Pay Attention to Slanderous Talks

One of the negative characteristics of some people is their speaking ill of each other. This characteristic is not only unpleasant by nature, but it is also a cause of much mischief. It causes suspicion, pessimism, disharmony, and strife among the people. It destroys friendly atmospheres and sows the seed of discord among families. It separates men from their wives and it could lead to homicide.

Unfortunately, this characteristic is so widespread among the people that it does not even seem bad any more. In a gathering it is rare not to hear gossiping and backbiting. Specially, in a women's gathering, the element of gossip is dominant. When two women meet, they start gossiping. They talk slanderously of others as if it is a competition. They sometimes talk about their husbands. For instance, they discuss their looks or jobs, and nd fault with the other woman's husband. One woman would blame the other one for being married to; say a mechanic or a shoemaker.

If the husband is a driver she would say: "Your husband is always traveling, how can you cope with this?" If he is a butcher, she would say: "Your husband always smells of fat." If he is not earning much, she would say: "How do you live with such little money? Why did you marry him? Is it not a pity that you, with such a beauty, have married such a short and puny man? How did your parents allow you to do this? Were they fed up with you? You could have married any man you wished. Why did you choose this man? He does not take you anywhere, not the cinema, not the theatre, nowhere.

By the way, your husband is such a grim faced man. How can you live with him? How could you, with all your education, marry a peasant?"

Talks of this kind can be heard among a fairly large percentage of the female population of any society. Women who are used to this manner of speaking, as a matter of fact, do not think of the grave consequences which might follow. They do not think that their gossiping or picking up faults could lead to divorce or even murder.

Such women are truly demons in a human form. They are the enemies of families. They create strife among the families and turn their houses into dark and horrible dungeons. What should one do? This is a component of our societies. Even though Islam has rmly prohibited us from such deeds we are not prepared to give them up.

"The Prophet of Allah (S) stated: 'Oh! Those of you who claim to be Muslims, but failed to let faith enter into your hearts, do not speak ill of Muslims and do not nd faults with them. Whoever nd faults with people, then Almighty Allah will be doing just the same while looking into their faults; and in that case they would be disgraced among the people, even though they may remain in their own houses.'"[66]

These evil-character women may pursue one or many goals. They gossip for the sake of revenge in order to break up a family. They may do it because of jealousy or self-glorication. They might want to cover their own deciencies or deceive the simple women. They may want to pretend that they are sympathetic. They sometimes gossip for amusement and do not pursue any goal other than satisfying their distasteful desires. But what one can be sure of is that deeds of this kind are not committed in order to help others and that such acts could have disastrous effects.

---

[66] Bihar al-Anwar, vol 57, p 218

The readers have surely come across certain events which have occurred as the result of gossip. The following is such a case:

"A woman said in the court: 'Mr… used to talk behind my husband- in order to cause a clash between me and my husband. He used to tell me that my husband was not good enough for me and that he did not understand me or have any emotions. He always wanted me to get a divorce and marry him… As a result of his deluding suggestions I was misled and one day we, both together, killed my husband.'" [67]

Dear madam! Now that you have realized the evil intentions behind gossip and if you are interested in your husband and children, then do not be inuenced by the tongues of the human-shaped devils. Do not give in to their false friendship. Be sure they are not your friends, but your foes who want to see you breaking away from your family. Do not be simple and do not believe them. Try to nd their evil intentions through sagacity. Stop them immediately when they set out to criticize your husband. Do not be shy to tell them: "If you want us to remain friends, then stop talking about my husband. You do not have any right t to criticize him. I love him and there is nothing wrong with him."

Once they detect your love towards your husband and children, through the rmness of your tongue, then they may become disappointed with misleading you and you will not be disturbed again. Do not think that they would become upset, or that you would lose your friends. If they are your true friends, then they should not be hurt and should even thank you. If they are your enemies, then what is better than avoiding them. If you encounter those who are persistent in their evil act, then cut off your relationship with them.

---

[67] Ittela'at, 27th Aban, 1350 Solar Hijri

The Satisfaction of Your Husband and Not Your Mother

A girl, while in her parents' house, is duty-bound to satisfy them. However, once she is married, her role changes.

In her husband's house, a woman should give priority to her husband's needs. Even when there are conicting desires of her husband and her parents, she should obey her husband, even at the expense of the parents' dissatisfaction. Disobedience to one's husband may harm one's marital relationship and vice-versa. Moreover, many mothers do not enjoy a proper education and wisdom.

Some mothers have not yet realized that they should leave their daughters to reach an understanding with their husbands of their own. The married couple must be left to plan their own affairs and if they encounter any difculty, they should overcome it through their own initiative.

Since the wives' mothers are unaware of this point, then, in their own minds, they try to make their son- in-law act according to their desires. They try, directly and indirectly, to interfere in their family affairs.

They use their young daughters, who are inexperienced and not quite aware of their situations, in order to inuence the sons-in-law. The mothers constantly tell their daughters how to act, what to do, what to say, and what not to say. The poor daughter, who regards her mother as sympathetic and experienced, obeys her and commits herself to the mother's desires too.

There would not be any problems if the son-in-law submits to the mother-in-law's desires: However, if he shows resistance, then rows begin to take shape. In the latter case the ignorant mother may become so stubborn that it may lead to the destruction of her daughter's family life. The ignorant mother, instead of encouraging her daughter to devote herself to her husband, makes her oppose her husband. The mother may tell her daughter:

"You have ruined your life. What an awful husband! What good men were prepared to marry you! What a good life your cousin has! How lucky your sister is! What have they got that you haven't? Why should you live like this? My poor daughter!"

The mother, whose words are regarded as sympathetic, causes family rows and arguments between the daughter and her husband. The daughter is placed in a situation to pick up rows with her husband. The parents would also take sides with her and nally in order to win the ght, they show willingness towards their daughter getting a divorce.

"A thirty-year old woman attacked her fty-year old mother for she had caused her divorce. This woman said: 'My mother talked behind my husband so much that it caused many arguments between me and him. Finally, I got divorced but soon regretted it. But it was too late, because six hours after our divorce, my former husband was engaged to my cousin. I was so frustrated that I decided to beat up my mother.'"[68]

"A thirty-nine year old man ran away from his wife and mother-in-law and left a letter saying: 'Because of my wife's attitude and because she was not prepared to go to Abadan with me, I decided to leave this world. My wife and her mother are responsible for my death'. Thus a man, who was fed up with his mother-in-law's interference, committed suicide.'" [69]

"A man, who was fed up with his mother-in-law's interference, threw her out of a taxi.'"[70]

Undoubtedly, daughters who obey mothers of this kind and submit to their wills, would inict an irreversible blow on themselves.

Therefore, any woman who cares for her family, should not be

---

[68] Ittela'at, 9th Azar, 1348 Solar Hijri.

[69] Ibid, 12th Urdibahisht, 1349 Solar Hijri

[70] Ibid, 13th Urdibahisht, 1349 Solar Hijri

inuenced by her mother's will and should not regard them as one hundred percent correct.

A wise and clever woman would always examine the suggestions and sayings of her mother before implementing them in her family life. She should implement them if they did not contradict or endanger her family bonds. In this case, the daughter should submit to the will of her mother. Otherwise, if the daughter reaches the conclusion that her mother is ignorant and her suggestions lead to rows and arguments, then she can reject her.

Anyway, there are two choices for the daughter:

1. To go along with the desires of her mother in which case, family arguments would follow; or
2. To ignore her mother, and comply with her husband's desires.

Obviously, one would not choose the former because if one did, then she would either have to live in a misery with her husband or divorce him. If she continues to live with her husband, then she, along with her husband, and the children, would suffer .In the case of divorce she would probably have to go to live with her parents. In this case they would not accept her as a member of the family and would try to get rid of her. She would be degraded and humiliated before all the other members of the family .It is also not easy to live alone. It will also not be easy to marry again. How can one be sure that the next round will be any better What about the children? What about the children of the next man? She might end up so frustrated that she might kill herself. She may become so difcult to live with that the next man she marries, may run away from her, or even kill himself.

Once a woman ponders over the consequences of acting upon the selsh and foolish desires of her mother or others, then she should rmly decide to ignore all the talk as not to endanger her relationship with her husband.

She could tell her mother:

"Now that I am married, it is better for me to try to protect my marriage, and keep my husband satised. I would rather treat him kindly, because he is my partner. He can make me happy and is able to help me. He shares ail the ups and downs of life with me. He is my choice and, if we have any difculties, we will try to solve them ourselves. We can plan our lives. Your interference may make a bad situation worse. If you want us to have a good relationship with you, then do not interfere in our lives, do not talk behind my husband, otherwise I will have to cut off my relationship with you."

If your mother, as a result of your suggestion, stops interfering, then you will not be disturbed. However, if she is not prepared to take any notice of you r desires, it would be better for you to stop seeing her. In this way you will be saved and you can live comfortably.

While, as a result of breaking away from you r parents, you may lose some of your respect among you r family, you will have earned many times over more respect from your husband.

"The Prophet of Allah (S) stated: 'The best of your women is one who gives birth to many children, is loving and chaste, who does not submit to the will of her relatives but is obedient towards her husband, adorns herself only for her husband and protects herself from strangers, listens to her husband and obeys him, accedes to his wishes in privacy and does not lose her modesty in any case."

"The Prophet (S) then added: 'The worst of your women is she who obeys her relatives but does not submit to the wishes of her husband, is barren and vindictive, is not afraid of committing bad deeds, adorns herself in the absence of her husband, would not accede to the wishes of her husband in privacy, would not accept his excuses and would not forgive his mistakes.'"[71]

Be Clean and Beautiful at Home Also

It is customary with most women that whenever they go to a party or a gathering, they wear their best dresses and adorn themselves with the best. However, upon returning home, they take their dresses off and put on an old and shabby dress. These women are not particular about cleanliness at home and do not beautify themselves. They walk around the house with disheveled hair, stained clothes, and torn socks. In fact, the situation must almost be reverse, that is, a woman should adorn herself at home and charm her husband in order to conquer his heart and in order not to leave any gap for other women to ll. Why should she look beautiful for others? Is it proper for a woman to expose her beauty before the eyes of other men and to create problems for the youth?

"The Prophet (S) of Islam stated: ' Any woman, who perfumes herself and leaves the house, is deprived from the blessings of the Almighty Allah until she returns home.'"[72]

"The Prophet (S) also stated: 'The best of your women is one who is obedient towards her husband, adorns herself for her husband but does not reveal her adornment to strangers; and the worst of your women is one who adorns herself in the absence of her husband.'"[73]

Dear Madam! Winning the heart of a man, especially for a long time, is not easy. Do not think: "He loves me. I don't need to look beautiful for him or try to win his heart or entice him." You must always maintain his love towards yourself. Be sure that your husband

---

[71] Bihar al-Anwar, vol 103, p 235

[72] Bihar al-Anwar, vol 103, p 247

[73] Ibid, p 235

would enjoy having a tidy beautiful and clean wife, even though he may not express it. If you do not satisfy his inner desires and do not dress attractively at home, he may see beautiful and attractive women out of the house. He may then become disheartened in you and might deviate from the right path. When he sees attractive women, he compares you with them. If you are an untidy, careless, and disheveled woman, he would think that other women are angels who have descended from the heavens. So try to look attractive at home and be sure that he will not lose interest in you.

Read the following letter written by a husband:

One cannot distinguish my wife from my servant in the house. I swear by Allah that I sometimes think: I wish she would wear one of these dresses made for parties, at home. I wish she would throwaway those torn and worn out clothes. I have told her a few times: 'darling! at least wear those nice dresses at home on holidays.' She told me sourly: 'I don't need to be particular when I am at home; but if one day I look untidy in the presence of my colleagues, then it would be embarrassing for me.'"

The reader might believe that while house keeping and cooking, a woman cannot dress up or look beautiful. This may be true but a housewife can have different clothes for doing the housework; and she can change her working clothes to proper ones while she is in the presence of her husband or for when he returns home. You can always comb your hair and keep yourself clean after the housework.

"Imam Baqir (a.s.) stated: 'It is incumbent upon a woman to perfume herself, to wear her best clothes, to adorn herself in the best way, and to meet her husband in this state day and night.'"[74]

"Imam as-Sadiq (a.s.) stated: 'Women should not give up adornment, be it only with a necklace. She should not have untinged hands, be it

---

[74] Shafi, vol 2, p 138

with a little henna. Even old women should not give up adornment.'"[75]

Be a Mother to Him

At the time of preoccupation and illness, one needs to be nursed by others. A nurse can assist the recovery of an ill person tremendously through kindness and loving care. Men are small children who have grown up. They still need motherly care. When a man gets married to a woman, he expects her to be a mother to him at times of illness and difculty.

Dear Madam! If your husband becomes ill, take care of him more than usual. Express your sympathy and pretend that you are extremely upset with this sickness. Console him, prepare all his requirements and keep the children quiet in order to keep him relaxed. If he needs a doctor or medicine, then act accordingly.

Cook the food he likes, and which is good for him. Ask about his health frequently. Try to stay by his bedside, as much as possible. If he is in so much pain that he cannot sleep, stay up with him, as much as possible. Once you wake up, go to him. Ask how is he. If he had not slept that night, then express your sorrow. Keep his room silent in the daytime. Your care for him would help him recover faster. He would appreciate your efforts and would love you more. Besides he would do the same for you if you ever became ill.

"The Prophet of Allah (S) stated: 'The Jihad of a woman is to care for her husband well.'"[76]

---

[75] Bihar al-Anwar, vol 103, p 228

[76] Bihar al-Anwar, vol 103, p 247

Keep the Secrets

Women usually like to know about their husbands' secrets, their earnings, their decisions about the future, and their work. They expect men not to hide anything from them.

On the contrary men are not willing to tell their wives everything. As a result, some husbands and wives constantly argue over this matter.

Some women say that their husbands do not trust them; do not let them read their letters; do not tell them the amount of their earnings; are not straight with them; do not answer their questions properly; and sometimes lie.

Incidentally, men do not mind telling their secrets to their wives. But they believe that their wives do not keep secrets; that they relate to others everything they know, and might even cause trouble for their husbands.

If one intends to nd out the secrets of others, it sufces for one to call on their wives. Some wives, by knowing their husbands' secrets, blackmail them, and thus misuse their husbands' trust in them.

Obviously men, up to a certain extent, have a point. Women, in comparison with men, are more under the inuence of their emotions. When women become angry, it would be difcult for them to control themselves, and by knowing their husbands' secrets, they could put their men in trouble.

Therefore, if a woman is interested in knowing her husband's secrets, she must be very careful not to speak of them anywhere without his permission. She must not even tell her best friends or relatives. It is not keeping a secret if you tell someone about it, and ask him not to repeat it to anybody, otherwise everyone will nd out about it.

Therefore a wise person is one who does not tell his secret to anyone. "Imam Ali (a.s) stated: 'The chest of a wise man is the safe for his secrets.'"[77]

"Imam ' Ali (a.s) also stated: 'The benevolence of this world and the next is in two things: keeping secrets, and friendship with the good people; and all the evils are in two things: revealing secrets, and keeping bad company.'"[78]

Accept His Management

Every institution, factory, and organization needs a responsible manager. In any sociological unit and organization, cooperation between the staff is important. However, running the affairs of such a unit needs a manager who can coordinate the duties.

One of the very important social units is the 'family'. Running the affairs of this unit is very vital and difcult.

Undoubtedly, there must be a deep understanding, and cooperation among the members of a family, but there must also be a manager who can act responsibly with regard to the family matters. Needless to say, if a family does not enjoy a person who can organize others it would suffer from disorder and chaos. Thus, either the husband must act as the director and the wife follows, or vice versa.

However, since the logical aspect of men is dominant over their emotional aspect, they can be better managers.

The Almighty Allah states in the Holy Qur'an:

> **"Men are the maintainers of women because Allah has made some of them to excel others and because they spend out of their money; the good women are therefore obedient..." (The Holy Qur'an, 4:34).**

---

[77] Bihar al-Anwar, vol 75, p 71

[78] Ibid, vol 74, p 178

Thus it is in the interest of the members of a family to regard the man as their guardian and the one in charge, and to seek his supervision in their deeds.

However, one should not conclude that the status of a woman in the house is belittled, but it is a fact that maintaining the order and discipline in the house requires the management of the husband. Women, who can think without being biased, would conrm this act.

"A woman said: 'We had a good tradition in Iran which has unfortunately faded away gradually. In this tradition the man used to be in charge of the family affairs. He used to be the boss. Nowadays, however, the situation is changed, and families cannot make their minds up as to who should be in charge. I believe that the woman of today, who more or less have the same social status as men, should accept her husband as the chief of the house… This old tradition has to be recommended to today's young woman, who intends to marry. She should enter her husband's house wearing a wedding dress and come out of it wearing a shroud.'"[79]

It is true that the everyday preoccupations of life do not allow man to participate in all the family affairs and that in practice the wife runs the house according to her desires, but nevertheless, the right of directorship remains with the man, and as such he should be respected.

Therefore, should a man express his opinion about any point in the household matters or suggest any thing, the wife should not oppose him or deny him his right of directorship in any way. Otherwise, the man would regard himself as powerless and look upon his wife as an impolite and ungrateful woman. He might hold a grudge against her and, at a later stage, even resist his wife's lawful wishes.

"The Prophet of Allah (S) stated: ' A good woman would pay heed to

---

[79] Ittela'at, 17th Murdad, 1351 Solar Hijri.

her husband's wishes and would act according to his desires.'"⁸⁰

"A woman asked the Prophet (S) of Allah: 'What is the duty of a woman with regard to her husband?' The Prophet (S) stated: 'She must obey him and must not violate his orders.'"⁸¹

"The Prophet of Allah (S) also stated: 'The worst of women is one who is stubborn and obstinate.'"⁸²

"The Prophet of Allah (S) also stated: 'The worst of women is one who is barren, dirty, obstinate and disobedient.'"⁸³

Dear Madam! Accept the authority of your husband. Seek his supervision in your household affairs. Do not violate his orders. Do not resist or oppose his participation in the household and family matters. Do not reject his participation even in those matters that you have more expertise. Do not practically make him powerless. Let him participate in your work occasionally. Teach your children to respect his authority, and ask them to get permission from their father in their affairs. Your children must learn not to violate his orders from an early age. This way your children will be brought up as obedient to their parents.

Be Resourceful when Times are Hard

Life is full of ups and downs. The wheels of fortune do not always rotate according to our desires. One goes through many difcult times. Everyone becomes ill. Many lose their jobs, and some may lose all their wealth. Many unpleasant incidents happen in the lives of everyone.

A man and a woman, who have sworn allegiance to each others and

---

[80] Bihar al-Anwar, vol 103, p 235

[81] Ibid, p 248

[82] Mustadrak, vol 2, p 532

[83] Shafi, vol 2, p 129

signed a covenant of marriage, should walk along the path of life hand in hand. The covenant should be so firm that it could hold them together in sickness and in health, in richer and poorer, and in good as well as bad times.

Dear Madam! If your husband becomes poor, must you add to his problems by having disagreeable behaviour. If he becomes ill, and bed-ridden, either at home or in the hospital, it is fair for you to increase your kindness towards him. You must nurse him, attend to his needs, and spend money for him. If you have money of your own you must pay for his treatment. Remember if you were ill, he would have paid for your health. Must you withhold your wealth in preference to your husband's health? If you fail to satisfy him at sensitive times like this, then he will be disappointed with you, and may even prefer to divorce you.

Here is a case to read about:

"A person came to the court to divorce his wife. He said: 'I became ill a few days ago and my doctor told me that had to have an operation. I asked my wife to lend me the money that she had saved. She disagreed and left my house. As a result, I had my operation in a state hospital. Now that I have my health back I am not prepared to live with a woman who prefers her money to her husband. How can one call this woman a 'wife'?"[84]

Every conscientious person would acknowledge that, in the above-mentioned case, it was the man who was right. Such a woman, who is not prepared to spend her money for the treatment of her husband, does not deserve the respected position of 'wifehood'.

Dear Madam! Be careful not to act mercilessly at a time when your husband suffers from a permanent illness; must you leave him and your children? How can you desert a man with whom you have had

---

[84] Ittela'at, 25th Azar, 1350 Solar Hijri

many joyful days and nights? How do you know that a similar fate is not awaiting you? How can you be sure that another man will be any better? Do not be stubborn and selsh. Be sacricial and devote yourself or the sake of Allah as well as your honour and children. Be patient and teach your children a lesson of devotion, love, and patience. You can be sure that, in this world and the next, you will be rewarded handsomely. Your devotion is the best way of showing your care for your husband which is placed at the same level as Jihad.

"The Prophet of Allah (S) stated: ' Jihad of a woman is in taking care of her husband.'"[85]

Do not Refuse to Talk and do not Sulk

It is customary with some women that, when upset with their husbands, they sulk, refuse to talk, do not attend to household work, do not eat, hit the children, or grumble. They believe that, not speaking, or quarrelling are the best possible ways of revenging their husbands. This attitude, not only fails to punish the man, but may result in his retaliation. Life then becomes difcult turning into a series of quarrels. The woman moans, then the man does. The woman refuses to talk and the man retaliates. The woman does something else, and the man does the same until they become tired and, through the mediation of relatives or friends, reconcile. But this is not the only time they had a row. There will be other occasions and there will be a few more days of bitterness.

Therefore, spending a lifetime of family rows will not be pleasant for either the parents or the children. Most of the runaway youth come from these kinds of families who then turn to crime and corruption.

"A youth, who was arrested on charges of theft, blamed his parents

---

[85] Bihar al-Anwar, vol 103. p 247

for his crime and said: 'My parents used to argue everyday after which they used to go to their relatives and I used to go into the streets and wander about. I was then deceived by others and later committed theft.'"[86]

"A ten-year old girl told the social workers: 'I remember vaguely that one night my parents argued over something. The following day, my mother left and a few days later, my father took me to my aunt. After a while an old woman took me from my aunt's house and brought me to Tehran. It is a few years now, that I have been living with her and I suffered so much that I do not want to go back to her.'"

"The teacher of a girl said: 'She is one of my students. She has not been performing well in her studies and looks to be suffering from something. She is always thinking. She has even been sitting in the courtyard of the school unprepared to go back home.' Two days ago I asked her: 'Why she was not going home?' She replied that she was living with an old woman who was nasty to her, and that she did not want her to returned home. I asked about her parents and she said they were separated.'"[87]

Dear madam! You should remember that if your husband reacts harshly towards you for not speaking with him, then he might even resort to severe measures such as hitting you. You would probably leave you r house to go to your parents' as the result of his harsh reaction. Next your parents would interfere and the row s between your husband and you would widen. You might end up getting a divorce in which case you would lose more than your husband. You might have to live on your own for the rest of your life. You will certainly regret a divorce.

"A woman said: 'I got married some time ago. I did not know much about caring for my husband and he did not know much about looking

---

[86] Ittela'at, 4th Azar, 1348 Solar Hijri.

[87] Ibid, 28th Mehr, 1348 Solar Hijri.

after me. We used to have row everyday. One week I wasn't talking and the week after he was refusing to speak to me.

Only on Fridays, through the mediation of friends and relatives, we used to be on good terms. Gradually, my husband became disappointed with me and thought of divorcing me and remarrying. Since I was young I was not prepared to change and did not object to a divorce. We got divorced and I rented a at. Soon I realized the dangers. Most of the people, whom I met, were out to deceive me. I decided to reconcile with my former husband and called at his house. There I met a lady who introduced herself as his wife. I cried all the way back to my house. I regretted my divorce, but it was too late.'"[88]

"A twenty-two year old woman who, after getting divorced, had taken her child to her parents, tried to commit suicide on the night of her sister's wedding.'"[89]

Dear Madam! You should seriously avoid sulking and not talking to your husband. If you are upset with him, be patient. Once you are calm and collected, talk .to him gently about your annoyance with him.

You can tell him, for instance, "You insulted me yesterday, or you rejected my demand... Is it fair that you should treat me in this way?"

Such an approach, not only relaxes you within, but also would admonish him. He would then try to make up for his wrongdoing, and would respect you for you r good manners. As a result, he would review his behaviour, and would try to discipline himself.

The Prophet of Allah (S) stated:

"At a time when two Muslims refuse to talk to each other and do not reconcile within three days, both will be out of Islam, and there will not remain any friendship between them. Then anyone of them who takes the initiative to reconcile with the other, would enter Paradise

---

[88] Ibid, 8th Azar, 1350 Solar Hijri

[89] Ibid, 17th Esfand, 1348 Solar Hijri

faster (than the other) on the Day of Judgment.'"⁹⁰

Remain Silent when he is Angry

A man meets many people while at work and he comes across many problems. Once he returns home from work, he is tired and upon confronting the smallest unpleasant incident becomes angry and may insult his family.

A wise lady would remain silent towards her husband's ranting and insults. The man would then calm down and would regret his insults. If he sees that there is not any reaction to his anger, he would even apologize. With this approach the family gets back to a normal situation after only an hour or two.

However, if the woman of the house did not understand her husband's sensitive position, then she would shout, swear, curse, and react sharply.

With this approach, the husband and wife might end up ghting and eventually resort to a divorce. Many families are broken up as the result of such little incidents. There are even cases where men become so angry that they erupt like a volcano and commit murder.

"A man shot himself, his wife and step-mother to death. The couple were believed to have had many rows and arguments right from the start of their marriage. On the night of the incident the husband had returned home from work when the couple started yet another argument. The husband hit his wife, and she decided to go to the police. Suddenly, the man took his gun, killed his wife, his step-mother, and then ended his own life with a bullet.'"⁹¹

Would it not have been better for the woman to have remained

---

[90] Bihar al-Anwar, vol 75, p 186

[91] Ittela'at, 17th Tir, 1349 Solar Hijri

silent at the husband's anger? Would three lives have been ended if the woman had been patient and had not reacted? Which one would you prefer? A few moments of silence or all the grave consequences of getting back at your husband?

Do not imagine for a second that the position of the man is being defended here and that he is not guilty. Not at all. Of course he is guilty. He should not vent his anger out on his family. In the next chapter, this point will be discussed in more detail but here we are saying that a woman should be wise and not react towards her husband's anger, be it right or not. In this situation, the man may not be able to control himself, so it is important that the wife, in order to save her family, remains silent.

Women usually think that remaining silent, when coming face to face with their husband's anger, would belittle them, and that they would lose their respect. However, the situation is quite the reverse. A man who sees no reaction when insulting his wife. Would certainly become remorseful. He would regard his wife as a loving woman, who despite her ability to retaliate, preferred to forgive him. His love for his wife would increase many fold. He would apologize and thus his wife would earn more respect.

The Prophet (a.s) of Allah stated: ' Any woman who tolerates her husband's bad temper, will be rewarded by Allah in the same way that He rewarded Asiyah[92], daughter of Muzahim.'"[93]

'The Prophet of Allah (S) stated: 'The best of your women is one who, upon seeing her husband's anger, tells him: 'I submit to your will. Sleep will not pass over my eyes unless you become content with me.'"[94]

'The Prophet of Allah (S) stated: 'Forgiveness and tolerance would

---

[92] Asiyah was the wife of Pharaoh.

[93] Bihar al-Anwar, vol. 103, p 247

[94] Ibid, p 239.

increase the honour and respect of their owners. Be forgiving so that Allah will cherish you.'"[95]

Men's Hobbies

Some men like to have certain hobbies at home. They are interested in, say, collecting stamps or books, gardening or photography in their spare time at home.

Such hobbies are classied as the best and healthiest pastime activities. They are very useful in that they attract men towards their homes as well as causing their relaxation. One can become depressed and frustrated from being idle. It is a fact that one of the ways of treating people with mental disorders is to keep them busy with certain jobs. Those of us who work more than others are generally less affected by mental disorders, and are less attracted towards dangerous occupation.

Therefore, woman should respect the healthy hobbies of their husbands and should not regard their pastime activities as foolish, cheap, and useless. Women must encourage their men in these activities and cooperate with them if necessary.

Housekeeping

A house, although a little place, is a precious blessing. It is a shelter for the man who takes refuge in it after the work. It is a place for seeking comfort in even after being on a holiday; one nds rest in one's home. No where is like home and nowhere can one nd peace as one would in one's home. It is a place of friendship, love, sincerity, comfort, rest, and a place where men and women of good virtue are educated and trained. It is a workshop to train mankind and a place to educate and

---

[95] Ibid, vol 71, p 419

bring up children. It is a little society from which greater societies are formed.

It is responsible for the advancement as well as the decline of the larger society. The small family environment. Although a part of a greater society, enjoys an internal independence, and that is why correcting a nation must start by improving the family. The responsibilities of education, training, and running of this sensitive social base lies with the women. Therefore women, through their deeds and behaviour towards their family, can determine the deterioration or progress of a nation. Thus, the job of a housewife is sensitive, respectable and revered.

Those who underestimate the family unit and are ashamed with this job, are in fact ignorant of its values.

A housewife should be proud of her position. She is holding a position of honour and sacrice for the good of society.

The educated women have a greater responsibility in this job, and thus should be models to others. They should practically prove that being educated does not contradict the position of being a housewife, but that it also helps in being a better housewife.

The educated woman should manage the family life in the best possible manner. She should be proud of housekeeping and should prove that an educated housewife is much better than an uneducated one.

It is not proper for her to abandon housework on the pretext of being educated. Education is not meant to shirk one's responsibilities, but it should help one perform his responsibilities better.

"A man, married to a high-school passed girl, said in the court: 'My wife refuses to do any housework. Every time I protested she said that housekeeping was not meant for an educated woman. She is not prepared to change and even asks me to divorce her, and marry a maid instead! Two nights ago I invited my wife's relatives and friends for dinner. At dinner time I spread the table cloth and placed my wife's framed certicate of high school in the middle. I then told everyone to observe the dinner that my wife prepares for me every night.'"[96]

Now let us read the opinion of a few educated women about being a housewife:

"Mrs. F. N. Shamirani, a graduate, said: 'A housewife should be an expert in dealing with the household affairs, a good companion for her husband, a good mother to her children and a good hostess to the guests.'"

"Dr Mrs Fasihi, pediatrician, said: 'I believe that a genuine housewife is one who is not engaged in ofce work, because ofce jobs in our country lack the necessary facilities regarding nutritional needs and nurseries. A woman in an ofce is always worried about her children or her husband's food.'"

"Mrs. S. Yakita, Technical Superintendent of the Faculty of Medicine, said: 'A housewife should be able to create a clean and attractive house with the least possible budget. She should share the happy and sad time with her husband. She must not ignore her husband's mental and social status.'"

"Mrs. I. Naimi said: ' A housewife is one who minimizes her unnecessary recreations and who would try to improve the affairs of the house. She must also be able to regulate the income with spending.'"[97]

Cleanliness

One of the important duties of a housewife is maintaining cleanliness in the house. Cleanliness is the key to hygiene and health. It prevents

---

[96] Ittela'at, 3rd Azar, 1350 Solar Hijri.

[97] Ittela'at, 28th Farwardin, 1351 Solar Hijri

many illnesses and attracts the family members to the house. It is a source of respect for the family.

"The Prophet of Allah (S) stated: 'The religion of Islam is based upon cleanliness.'" [98]

"The Prophet of Allah (S) also stated: 'Islam is immaculate, so you should make efforts for cleanliness because only the clean ones would enter Paradise.'"[99]

Always keep your house clean and tidy. Dust it off once a day and remove all stains and dirt from the walls, doors, windows, furniture, and other items. Keep the garbage in a covered dustbin; keep it away from the other rooms, and kitchen. Empty the dustbin regularly. Do not keep the garbage in front of your house. Do not let your children urinate in the garden or the yard, and if they did, wash the place immediately. Dirt is a center for dangerous microbes. Do not pile up dirty dishes. Wash them as soon as possible. Do not forget that deadly germs grow on dirt and can become fatal to you and your family.

Wash the dishes with clean water, and afterwards keep them in a clean place. Remove all dirty clothes, especially babies' nappies, from the vicinity of all rooms and kitchen and wash them as soon as possible.

Keep all the family clothes, especially the underwear, clean and tidy. Wash the meat, vegetables and all your food ingredients before cooking. Wash all fruits before eating them because some fruits are sprayed with poisonous substances.

Wash your hands before eating and teach your children to do the same. After food, one should wash one's hands and mouth. If possible one should brush one's teeth after every meal. Brushing one's teeth is essential, at least, once a day, preferably before sleeping at night.

Cut your nails once a week. Long nails are not hygienic, because

---

[98] Mahajjat al-Bayda, vol 1, p 166

[99] Majma' al-Zawaid, vol 5, p 132

germs can live under long nails. Take a bath, at least, once a week, or if possible every other day.

One must remove all hair from under one's armpit as well as other places by shaving or other means. Hidden hair on the body is a suitable place for the growing germs. Do not leave food exposed to ies, because ies are carriers of many dangerous microbes.

The holy religion of Islam strongly recommends people to observe cleanliness.

"Imam as-Sadiq (a.s) stated: 'Almighty Allah likes adornment, being beautiful, and nds the pretention of being poor as distasteful. He likes to see the effects of his blessings upon his worshipper, that is to see him clean, tidy and using scent, to decorate his house, to dust off his house environment, to turn the lights on before sunset -because this deed takes away the poverty from home and increases sustenance.'"[100]

"The Prophet of Allah (S) stated: ' A dirty person is a bad servant (to Allah).'"[101]

"Imam Ali (a.s) stated: 'Keep your house clean of spider's webs, because a spider's web is a cause of poverty.'"[102]

"The Prophet of Allah (S) stated: 'Do not leave the rubbish inside the house at night, because Shaytan (Satan), i.e. pollution and uncleanliness takes its abode there.'"[103]

"The Prophet of Allah (S) also stated: 'One's clothes must always be clean.'"[104]

"In addition, the Prophet of Allah (S) stated: 'Do not leave an oily

---

[100] Bihar al-Anwar, vol 79, p 300

[101] Shafi, vol 1, p 208

[102] Bihar al-Anwar, vol 76, p 175

[103] Ibid

[104] Shafi, vol p 208

cloth in the house, because Satan takes its abode there.'"¹⁰⁵

"Imam as-Sadiq (a.s) stated: 'Washing dishes and cleaning around the house increases the sustenance.'"¹⁰⁶

"Imam as-Sadiq (a.s) also stated: 'Do not leave the dishes without a cover, otherwise Satan spits at them and uses them.'"¹⁰⁷

"In addition, Imam as-Sadiq (a.s) stated: 'Fruits are sprayed with poisonous substances, so wash them before eating.'"¹⁰⁸

"Imam al-Kadhim (a.s) stated: 'Taking a bath every other day would fatten one.'"¹⁰⁹

"The Prophet of Allah (S) stated: 'Do not leave the rubbish behind the front door of the house because Satan takes its abode there.'"¹¹⁰

"The Prophet of Allah (S) also stated: 'If it had not been something inconvenient for my followers, I would have ordered them to brush their teeth with every wudu (ablution) for prayer (i.e., ve times a day).'"¹¹¹

"Imam as-Sadiq (a.s) stated: 'Cutting one's nails on Fridays would prevent one from being affected by leprosy, insanity, alopecia and blindness.'"¹¹²

"It has been related that: 'Satan takes his sleep underneath the (long) nails.'"¹¹³

"Imam Ali (a.s) stated: 'Washing one's hands, before having meals,

---

[105] Ibid, p 215

[106] Bihar al-Anwar, vol 76, p 176

[107] Ibid

[108] Shafi, vol 2, p 124

[109] Ibid, vol 1, p 209

[110] Ibid, p 210

[111] Ibid, p 211

[112] Ibid

[113] Ibid

would prolong life, prevent one's clothes from becoming dirty and would enlighten one's eyes.'"[114]

A Tidy House

A tidy house is preferred to an untidy one in many ways.

Firstly, the tidiness helps the house look clean, attractive and beautiful, An arranged house, does not bore one, but would be a source of joy and happiness.

Secondly, the job of house-keeping would be easier in a well-ordered house, and the housewife, by knowing the exact location of the household contents, would not waste time to look for them. As a result the woman would not become tired with her job.

Thirdly, it attracts the man to his house and his wife. A well-ordered house is representative of the woman's quality.

Fourthly, a tidy house is a source of pride for the whole family. Whoever visits it, appreciates it, and admire the woman's talent and good taste.

Having many luxurious items would not beautify a house, but the manner in which the household contents are arranged, would make it attractive. You must have seen wealthy people whose house, despite containing many luxurious items, is boring, and there are poor people whose houses, because of being orderly, are enjoyable to look at.

Therefore, arranging a house is one of the duties of housewives. Talented ladies with good taste know how to put their houses in order, but mentioning a few points here may prove useful.

Classifying your dishes: Do not pile them all on top of each other. Leave all the cutlery in one place and place the dishes somewhere else. Put all the dishes for guests separate from the dishes you use everyday.

---

[114] Ibid, vol 2, p 123

Do the same for every thing else. Every thing must be put in its proper place so that all the family members are able to nd them, even in the dark.

Some ladies may believe that such a program suits the rich and the wealthy .But this is not correct, even poor people should arrange their belongings, including their dishes, beds, and clothes. For instance, the wife should keep her own clothes separate from her husband's and her children's. The winter clothes must be separate from summer ones. Dirty clothes must have their own place. The ornaments must be put in their proper locations. Teach your children to be tidy with their clothes, books, toys, etc. You can be certain that by being tidy, your children would learn and would follow you.

Untidy women blame their children for the house being in a state of mess, whereas it is the children who learn from their parents. If the parents are tidy, then the children would learn and children, by nature, are willing to be disciplined.

Keep all your money, important papers, documents, jewelry and certicates in a safe or a place out of the reach of children. It is not correct to punish a child for touching, destroying or losing any of the precious items that you have left within their reach. The parents are the guilty ones and they should know better.

"A man left some money with his wife and asked her to leave it in a safe place…, and then put it on the mantle piece and left the house. After a short while the man returned home and did not nd the money he had left. He looked around the house anxiously, and saw his ve-year old boy burning something in the garden. The mother of the boy angrily went up to him, lifted him up, and then threw him on the ground so hard that it killed the boy outright. She was quite scared while looking at her son's corpse when the man came out into the garden. He started hitting her, and then decided to go to the police. He got on his motorcycle, but on the way to the police station, he had an accident. He is now in the Intensive Care Unit.'" [115]

Who do you think, is guilty party in this incident? You can judge for yourself. Perhaps your know of a similar occurrence.

Medicines, parafn, petrol, and poisonous substances should always be kept out of the reach of children. Children drink and eat anything which looks like water and food. Do not endanger their lives by being careless. There are many children who die as the result of their parents' carelessness.

"Two children, a brother and a sister, aged 6 and 4 years drank a solution of DDT. The four-year old girl died, and her brother survived. The children were on their own in their house. They drank the solution in order to quench their thirst. Their mother said in the hospital that the solution was made to kill the mice in her house.'"[116]

"Two children drank kerosene, mistakenly thinking that it was water."
"Another child swallowed ten of her mother's tablets."
"All these children were taken to hospital for treatment."[117]

Finally, you are reminded that discipline is only useful up to a certain extent in that it should not deprive you from comfort. You should not be obsessed with tidiness, because obsession itself can cause problems:

"A man said: 'I am fed up with my wife's obsession with cleanliness and tidiness. Everyday when I return home at 4-30 pm, my wife makes me wash my hands and feet a few times. She wants me to put my clothes in their proper place. She doesn't even let me smoke in all the rooms. I have always lived freely, but during the four years of my marriage, I have been living in a prison. Why should one care for cleanliness and tidiness so much. This is an obsession and I hate obsession.'"[118]

---

[115] Ittela'at, 23rd Bahman, 1348 Solar Hijri

[116] Ibid, 26th Tir, 1351 Solar Hijri.

[117] Ibid, 11th Esfand, 1348 Solar Hijri.

[118] Ibid, 3rd Bahman, 1350 Solar Hijri

A moderate behaviour is the best in all aspects of one's life. One should not be so chaotic that it becomes impossible to live a normal life, and also one should not overindulge in cleanliness to the extent that it becomes an obsession.

Preparing Food

Another very important responsibility of a housewife is preparing food for her family. A good housewife is also a good cook who can prepare delicious food with little money, while a bad housewife cooks bad food with expensive ingredients. Delicious food is a means of attracting her husband towards her. A man whose wife cooks well, does not particularly enjoy eating out.

"The Prophet of Allah (S) stated: 'The best of your women is one who perfumes herself, prepares food skillfully and would not overindulge in spending. Such a woman is one of the workforce of Allah and a person who works for Allah would never have to face either regret or defeat.'"[119]

It is not possible for me to write down recipes, but there are many good books on the subject which can be obtained and used to cook delicious foods.

But just a few points to remember:

The purpose of eating is not to ll one's stomach but that it also supplies the body with all the nourishment it needs to continue its function. The necessary nourishment for the body is contained in meat, fruits, vegetables and cereals and can be classied into six groups:

1. Water,
2. Minerals, such as calcium, phosphorus, iron, copper, etc,

---

[119] Wasa'il al-Shiah, vol 14, p 15

3. Starchy substances (carbohydrates),
4. Fats,
5. Proteins, and
6. Vitamins like, A, B, C, D, K.

The majority of one's weight is water. Water dissolves the solid food in order to prepare it for absorption by the intestines. Water also regulates the body's temperature.

The minerals are necessary for the growth of bones, teeth, and the regulation of muscle functions. Carbohydrates create energy and heat.

Protein helps in the replacing of old or dead cells causing the growth of the body.

Vitamins are also important for the growth, strengthening the bones, regulating the chemical reactions in the body, and are vital in maintaining a healthy nervous system.

Each of the above substances is vital for the body. Malnutrition causes many illnesses and can be fatal. The quality of the food is important and has a proportional relationship with one's life span, happiness or sadness, beauty or ugliness and healthy nerves or mental disorders.

We are what we eat. If one monitors his food and cares for his eating habits, he would become ill less frequently. It is not wise to eat just delicious food without pondering over its quality. Once one's health is impaired as a result of bad food, one would have to seek medical treatment by a doctor, but unfortunately the human body would never be restored to its original health.

"The Prophet of Allah (S) stated: 'The stomach is the centre of all illnesses.'"[120]

Since the choice of food is with the women, therefore, they are very

---

[120] Bihar al-Anwar, vol 62, p 290

much responsible for the family health. The smallest carelessness on her part, would expose the health of all the family members to many illnesses.

Therefore a housewife, besides being a good cook, should be able to identify the quality of the food.

Firstly: She should make a food which has all the nourishment necessary for a human body to function properly.

"The Prophet of Allah (S) stated: 'The duty of a woman towards her husband is to turn the lights on in the house and to prepare good and suitable food.'"[121]

"A woman asked the Prophet (S) of Allah: 'What good (reward) is awaiting a woman who performs her duties in her husband's house?' The Prophet (S) stated: 'For every activity that she does concerning the household matters, Allah looks on her kindly, and whoever enjoys the grace of Allah would not be tormented.'"[122]

Secondly: The dietary needs of people are not the same. Age, size of the body and other possible factors determine the level of our nutritional requirements. For instance, a child, who is growing, need more calcium in comparison with a middle-aged person. The youth need more energy providing food because they have more activities.

One's job is also a factor in determining the type of food one should eat. For instance, a worker needs more fatty, sugary, and starchy food, because he is very active. . The weather is another factor. Our nutritional requirements differ from each other in the seasons of summer, and winter. Also an ill person would eat differently from a healthy one. A good cook should remember all these points.

Thirdly: It is a fact that when one reaches the age of forty and over, he is likely to get fat. Perhaps some people regard obesity as the sign

---

[121] Mustadrak, vol 2, p 551.

[122] Bihar al-Anwar, vol 103, p 251

of health, but they are mistaken. Obesity is an illness which could have very bad effects on the heart, blood pressure, kidneys, gall-bladder, liver, and may cause angina and diabetes.

Statistics coming from medical sources and insurance companies suggest rstly that thin people live longer than fat ones.

Beyond the age of forty, one becomes less active and thus needs less fat, sugar, and starch. The calories are not turned into energy as much as before and therefore contribute towards the fattening of the body. It is therefore better to reduce your consumption of these substances.

A woman who cares for her husband's health should put him on a special diet to stop him from getting fat. He should eat less sweets, fat, and cream, but more eggs, liver, poultry, red meat, sh and cheese. Dairy products are also useful. If permitted by the doctor, the overweight person should consume plenty of fruit, and vegetables.

If you are fed up with your husband, if you prefer to be a widow, or if you want to murder your husband without the risks of being prosecuted by the police -then you will not have to do much. Just put plenty of delicious and fattening foods before him. Encourage him to eat as much bread, rice and cakes as possible. Consequently you will get rid of him and not only will you become a widow but he would also thank you for feeding him with all these delicious foods.

You may suggest that such a program is possible for the wealthy people who can afford to buy any type of food they wish. You may think it impossible for those who are not so well off.

But one should not forget that all the nutritional values are hidden in the simple and natural foods. A woman who has learned about cooking would tell you that one could get all the nutritional requirements for the body from simple foodstuff such as fruits, cereals. Vegetables. and dairy products. One can cook a meal with these ingredients which is both hygienic, healthy, and cheap.

Receiving Guests

One of the inevitable tasks of every family is to entertain guests at one time or another. This is an enjoyable tradition as a result of which friendships become closer and people can forget their problems temporarily. Keeping company with friends and relatives is one of the healthiest pastimes.

"The Prophet of Allah (S) stated: 'The sustenance of a guest is descended from the heavens. and upon eating it, the sins of the host are forgiven.'"[123]

"Imam Reza (a.s) stated: ' A generous person eats the food offered to him by others so that they eat his.

But a miser would not eat the offered food by others lest they eat his.'"[124]

"The Prophet of Allah (S) stated: 'Associating with friends causes kindness (amongst them).'"[125]

"Imam Muhammad Taqi (a.s) stated: ' Associating with friends matures one's mind and enlivens one's heart, be it even only slightly.'"[126]

In the turbulent sea of life, one's soul needs tranquility, and this peace of mind can be found when keeping company with one's friends.

People would forget their problems while present in a friendly gathering. Not only can friendships become stronger, but it would serve to boost one's morale.

Entertaining guests is a good custom and rarely one would deny its merits, but there are two difculties with it that make some families reluctant to take part in this age-old tradition.

---

[123] Wasa'il al-Shi'ah, vol 16, p 557

[124] Ibid, p 520

[125] Bihar al-Anwar, vol 74, p 355

[126] Ibid, p 353

Part 1: The Duties of Women

First: Luxury goods and vying with one another has made life difcult for many of us. Household goods which are meant to serve our comfort have turned into a means of showing off and ostentation. Thus people are tending to associate less frequently with each other. Although many who are willing to socialize, refuse to do so, because they have the wrong idea that they do not possess many luxurious items in their homes that it would be better to keep away from others and save themselves the embarrassment. This reection destroys one's situation in the life after death as well as placing him in a difcult situation in this world.

Dear Madam! Do your friends come to your house in order to watch your luxury goods? If so, advise them to go to the stores and museums instead of coming to visit you. Associating with others is meant to increase one's friendship with them as well as having a pleasant time. It is not meant for showing off or lling one's stomach. Everyone is annoyed with 'luxurism' and rivalry of this kind. But they dare not dispose of this mistaken tradition.

If you were prepared to entertain your guests in a simple manner, you would see that they would follow you. This way you can associate with your friends simply and without going to too much trouble. Thus, the solution to this problem is easy .Instead of trying to match your belongings to those of others'; you should concentrate on strengthening the bonds of friendship with them through kindness.

Second: Another difculty is about the hosting of one's guests. A housewife goes through the trouble of making food for a few guests over a period of a few hours. Sometimes a woman cannot prepare a delicious meal, after which the husband may become upset. Her husband may also show his displeasure towards her cooking. Therefore, some parties are accompanied with the anxiety of the host couple as a result of which people tend to avoid having a party.

Of course it is true that holding a party is not easy, but the main difculty arises when the housewife does not have sufcient knowledge about how to look after her guests.

Hosting one's guests becomes easy if one is prepared to learn the necessary skills. Here two case studies are presented. You may follow whichever you prefer while entertaining your guests:

Case (a): The man informs his wife that on Friday night, ten of his friends are coming for dinner His wife who has had bitter experience with previous parties, suddenly becomes enraged and protests to her husband. After a detailed discussion and the husband's pleading, the reluctant wife agrees to arrange the dinner for his guests. They spend their days and nights in a certain air of restlessness, and excitement until Friday.

On Friday morning one of them goes for shopping. He remembers the necessary items to buy and after purchasing a few items, returns home.

The housewife starts her job after lunch. She suddenly confronts many problems. She has to do the cooking, washing, sweeping, dusting, arranging the guestroom, and so on. Also, she has to do all this and more on her own or at the most with only one person helping her. She begins to work with a great deal of worry. She looks for the knife to cut the onions, searches the house for salt, etc. She realizes that there is not any tomato in the house, so she sends somebody to buy it. She must then fry the chickens, cut the meat, soak the rice in water, clean the vegetables… etc.

She becomes touchy and nervous, and then shouts at the servant, curses her daughter, hits her son and then runs out of gas or kerosene. "Oh God! What shall I do?" she screams.

All of a sudden the door bell rings. The guests have arrived! They come in one after another. The poor husband, who is aware of wife's anxiety, welcomes the guests into the house and leads them to the sitting room. He then intends to serve them with tea, but he nds out that tea is not ready. He shouts at his daughter or son for not putting the kettle on the samovar.

Once the tea is made, he nds out that they do not have enough sugar. After having to buy some more sugar, he takes a few cups of tea to the guests. He looks at them but his mind is in the kitchen. He knows what is going on in that quarter. He cannot sit comfortably or talk to the guests peacefully. He is worried about the dinner. It is even worse if there are women among the guests in which case they keep asking where the woman of the house is. The man must answer that his wife is busy cooking and she will be with them soon.

The wife, occasionally goes to the guests but cannot stay and sit with them. She, while apologizing to them once again returns to her kitchen. It is not possible for her to prepare a really delicious meal under these conditions.

Once the meal is ready, she has to look for the dishes, make a drink, get the glasses, ll the salt and pepper shakers, etc.

The guests after eating their meal nally say 'good-bye' to their hosts and leave.

Conclusion: The meal was either too salty or salt less, burnt or less-cooked. Also some of the items may have been forgotten by the hostess, and therefore not placed before her guests.

It is now midnight and the wife is exhausted. She has not had a moment of rest since noon. Also she was unable to attend to the guests properly.

The husband has gone through a great deal of worry. He has spent a lot of money for the party, but the evening was not enjoyable and he may even blame his wife.

The couple, not only have not enjoyed the party, but may also have an argument over it, and may even decide not to hold any more parties.

The guests did not enjoy the party either, because they felt that they had caused a lot of trouble for their hosts and they probably wished that they had not come at all.

Undoubtedly, the readers would not enjoy such a situation and would not be prepared or willing to have this kind of experience.

Do you know what the source of this problem is? Well, the only real cause is the lack of experience and know-how of the housewife about how to entertain her guests. Otherwise, holding a party is not such a difcult task.

Now the second option:

Case (b): The man informs his wife that ten of their friends will be coming for dinner on Friday night. The wife responds by saying "Very well, what should we prepare for dinner that night?" The couple decides on this matter together and then writes down all the necessary items needed for the party. They recheck their needs again and by crossing out those items that they already have in their house, re-write the items that they would have to purchase. Then in good time they do their shopping.

On Thursday, a day before the party, they nish some of the work such as cutting onions, washing the potatoes, lling the salt and pepper shakers, preparing the table wares and so on.

The following morning, the woman of the house after eating breakfast, carries out some of her tasks like washing, cutting and frying the meat, chicken, and potatoes. After lunch she can take a rest after which she can nish the remainder of her work.

So she can nish all her cooking, tidying up and arranging the house without any rush or worries. There would be no need for arguments or any cause for confusion. She would have enough time to get herself ready and prepare a cup of tea when their guests arrive. She can then welcome the guests alongside her husband and sit and talk to them. She would just need to go to the kitchen to make sure everything was going smoothly.

She can ask her husband and the children to help her in setting the food in front of the guests. Therefore, everyone would be able to comfortably enjoy their delicious meal.

Conclusion: The guests have enjoyed the company of their hosts. They have talked and their friendship had become stronger. They have enjoyed the meal and have admired the housewife for her ability to entertain them. Finally, they have enjoyed an evening which they would remember for a long time to come.

The husband has been able to associate with the guests. He has had a good time with his friends and is happy with his wife for not letting him down. They become encouraged to invite their friends over and over again.

Finally, the woman who, through patience and know- how, has been able to entertain the guests normally and without any problem, is satised with herself. She feels happy with her husband and has proved herself to be a good hostess.

Now you can choose to follow either of the two examples.

The Trustee of the House

Men are usually the supporters of the family. They work hard and spend their earnings on their wives and children. They regard this as their duty and do not ever show their displeasure in their hardship.

But men also expect their wives to economize and not to spend their money extravagantly. The women are expected to classify the necessities and spend on the priorities such as food, clothes, medicine, rent, electricity, telephone, gas and water bills. Placing such items as luxury goods on the list of one's priorities is regarded as squandering and wasteful. Men do not like their wives to misuse their money in buying unnecessary goods or lavishly spending.

If a man nds his wife trustworthy of caring for his money, if he is sure that his wife does not spend lavishly and if he is certain that his hard earned money is not wasted away he would then work harder and would not waste his money.

On the other hand, if the woman spends the money on her clothes and adornment, or if she spends on unnecessary items and they would have to borrow in order to live, or if the family, like an indel enemy, plunders his wealth, then the man will become disheartened. He would lose interest in working and supporting his family. He would think it illogical to work and support the people who do not appreciate his efforts. He may even go astray and follow a corrupt path. It might shatter the foundations of the family.

Dear Madam! Although your husband's money and wealth is at your disposal, do not regard it as your own. The wealth is lawfully his and you are the trusted one. Therefore, taking any item into your possession, giving anything away, presenting or selling any of his belongings needs his permission. You are responsible for his wealth and as such you must protect it. If you shirk your responsibility, you would be questioned in the world Hereafter.

"The Prophet (a.s) of Allah stated: 'A woman is the protector and trustee of her husband's wealth and as such is responsible.'"[127]

"The Prophet of Allah (S) also stated: 'The best of your women is one who perfumes herself, prepares delicious food and would not overindulge in spending. Such a woman is a representative of and one of the workforce of Allah, and a person who works for Allah would never be faced with regret or defeat.'"[128]

"A woman asked the Prophet (S) of Allah: 'What are the rights of a husband over his wife?' The Prophet

(S) stated: 'She must be obedient towards him, must not violate his

---

[127] Mustadrak, vol 2, p 550

[128] Wasa.il al-Shiah, vol 14, p 15

orders and should not give away anything without his permission.'"[129]

"The Prophet of Allah (S) also stated: 'The best of your women is one who spends less.'"[130]

Careers of women

It is right that earning a family's living is an obligatory deed of the man, and that women are not Islamically (as per Islamic laws) responsible for this act. Women, however, should also have a job. In Islam, idleness is discredited and reproached.

"Imam as-Sadiq (a.s.) stated: 'The Almighty Allah hates too much sleep and too much rest.'"[131]

"Imam as-Sadiq (a.s.) also stated: 'Too much sleep wastes and ruins both one's worldly life and the religion (the life in the world Hereafter).'"[132]

"Hadrat Zahra (a.s) also used to work at home."[133]

Anyone, in need or not, should have a job. He should not waste his life by not doing anything, but he should work and offer his share in building a better world.

If necessary, one should spend his earnings for his family and himself, but if not needed then he should donate his earnings from work to those who need his help. Idleness is tedious and, more often than not, causes mental and psychological disorders, as well as moral corruption.

The best job for married women is to take care of the house. Housekeeping, childcare, etc are the best and the easiest jobs that

---

[129] Bihar al-Anwar, vol 103, p 248

[130] Mustadrak, vol 2, p 532

[131] Usul al-Kafi, vol 5, p 84

[132] Ibid

[133] Ibid, p 86

women can do.

A talented and hardworking housewife can turn her house into a heavenly place for her children and husband; and this is a valuable and worthwhile job.

"The Prophet (S) stated: 'A woman's Jihad is when she attends to her husband (and takes care of him well).'"[134]

"Umm-e-Salamah asked the Prophet (S): 'How much reward is there for a woman's housework?' The Prophet (S) replied: 'Any woman who, in the way of improving the order of the house, takes something from somewhere and places it somewhere else, would enjoy the grace of Allah, and whoever attracts the blessings of Allah, would not be tormented by Allah's anger'.

Umm-e-Salamah said: 'O Rasul-Allah (Messenger (SA) of Allah)! May my parents be sacriced for you, please state other rewards for women'. The Prophet of Allah (S) stated: 'When a woman becomes pregnant, Allah rewards her as much as He would to someone who goes for Jihad (holy war) with all his wealth and life. Then when she delivers her baby, a call would reach her stating 'all your sins are forgiven; start a new life again.' Each time she feeds her baby with her milk, Allah gives her reward equal to that of freeing a slave for each feeding.'"[135]

Housewives, even not busy with their housework, should nd something to do. They can read books, conduct research on something useful, and add to their knowledge and skills. They can write articles, and even books. They can engage in drawing, painting, tailoring, knitting, sewing, and so forth. As a result they can help their families economically as well as contributing to their society by making their achievements available to the public. Working prevents the development of many mental disorders.

---

[134] Bihar al-Anwar, vol 103, p 247

[135] Ibid, p 251

"Imam Ali (a.s) stated: ' Allah likes a pious person who is honestly engaged in doing a job.'"[136]

While some women work at home, there are others who prefer an outside job. This preference may be either for economical or other reasons. In this case, the best jobs are cultural occupations or nursing. Nurseries, primary and high schools are suitable places for women to train and teach female students. Hospitals are also suitable places where women can serve as nurses and doctors. Such jobs are agreeable to the female nature; and also, there would rarely, if at all, be the need for them to mix with or come across the men who are not mahram (near relatives with whom marriage is prohibited).

The following are recommendations to those ladies who intend to or who are working outside their homes:

1. Consult your husband before taking up a job. It is your husband's right to grant or refuse you permission to work. Starting to work without your husband's permission will be detrimental to the serenity and loving atmosphere of your family. Men are also advised not to be adamantly negative with regard to their wives' working outside the house, unless the job concerned is considered unsuitable for them.

2. Ladies should observe proper Islamic Hijab (veil) when not at home. They should go to work without any make up, and with plain clothes. They must avoid mixing with men who are not mahram as much as possible. An ofce is a place to work in and is not for the purpose of showing off, or for rivalry. Prestige and dignity does not come with what you wear, but what you do, and how well you do it. Be and act as a dignied Muslim woman. Maintain your self-respect, and do not hurt your husband's

---

[136] Usul al-Kafi, vol 5, p 113

feelings; save your adornments and your beautiful dresses for him at home.

3. Ladies should be aware that although they are working outside the house, they are still expected by their husbands and children to attend to such activities as housekeeping, cooking, washing, and so forth. This can be done by cooperation within the family. An outside job should not pave the way for upsetting the whole family. Men are also advised to help their wives with regard to housekeeping. Husbands should not expect their wives to work both outside and inside the house on their own. Such an expectation is neither lawful nor fair. Men and women should share the housework.

4. If a woman, who working outside has a child, then she should leave the child in a nursery or with someone trusted and kind. It is neither right nor wise to leave children at home on their own, since many children become fearful or helpless when they have to confront dangerous situations.

5. If a woman feels that, in addition to the above works and responsibilities, she should under take another job, then she should denitely come to an understanding with her husband and take up a job with his permission and under his advice. If the husband does not agree, she should forget about this job. If the husband agrees for the wife's undertaking a job, she must try to select a job in which she comes in contact with minimum number of strange men. This is in the interest of both herself and the society. In any case, while outside her home, she must certainly observe Islamic Hijab and see that she remains simple and without any make-up.

Do not Waste your Spare Time

The housework comprises of a great deal of work. If a housewife intends to carry out her job perfectly, she would not have enough time to do anything else. This is especially true if she has to take care of a few children as well. But most housewives do nd some spare time.

Everyone spends his spare time in one way or another. Some women waste their time. They might just walk in the streets or nd another woman to talk to. Most of the time their few hours of talking are not worth a penny. They would listen to repeated words which only prove to be time wasting and nerve breaking. Such idle chatting always results in one's moral degradation. The women who go through life in this way, are surely losers in this world and the next. How surprising it is that if anyone should lose some money, he would become very upset, but people do not give a thought about losing their precious moments of life.

A wise person would make the most out of his precious hours of life. What valuable achievements one can have!

Idleness is very harmful and is a cause of many mental disorders and anxieties. An idle person keeps thinking and nds ways of feeling sad. He would experience many types of worries after which his mind would become confused. A happy person is one who is busy doing something. An unlucky person is one who has excess idle time enough to think of the ups and downs of his life. Being busy is enjoyable, and idleness is a source of depression.

Is it not a pity that one should waste his precious life or spend some of its moments without getting anything in return?

Dear Madam! You can make the most out of your spare minutes or hours. You can do scienctic tasks. You can buy the related books and with the help of your husband, increase your knowledge. Any course is possible; physics, chemistry, Qur'an, philosophy, history, geography, literature, psychology, etc. You would enjoy it and perhaps you could one day contribute to your society through your knowledge. You can write articles or even books after which your name will remain. You can earn money too.

Do not think that this is too ambitious for a housewife. Do not imagine that all the great women of history have been sitting idle. They, too, were housewives but the ones who did not waste their spare time.

Mrs. Dorothy Carnegie was a housewife who wrote a good book. She used to do the housework and also helped her husband (Dale Carnegie) in writing his famous book "How to Make Friends and Inuence People". She writes in her book concerning principles of looking after the husband: "I have written this book during my child's two-hour sleep. I did a lot of my reading during the time my hair were getting dried in the hairdressing saloon."

There are many women who have been writing great books or have had many achievements in scientic elds.

If you are an enthusiastic person, you could be one of them.

If your husband is a researcher, then help him in his eld. Is it not a pity for an educated woman to give up all her knowledge?

"Imam Ali (a.s) stated: 'There is not any better treasure other than knowledge.'"[137]

"Imam Baqir (a.s) stated: 'Whoever spends his day and night in seeking knowledge, would surely be enjoined by the blessings of Allah.'"[138]

If you are not interested in reading or research then keep yourself busy with handicraft or artistic hobbies such as dress making, painting, knitting, ower decorations, etc.

---

[137] Bihar al-Anwar, vol 1 p 165

[138] Ibid, p 174.

You can learn such arts and practice them. These skills may help you mentally and nancially. Islam has also proposed handicraft to women in their spare time. The Prophet of Allah (S) stated: "Spinning (and weaving) is a good pastime for women."[139]

Motherhood (Caring for Children)

One of the important duties of women is caring for their children. This is not an easy task but one which is very sensitive and vital. It is the most sacred and most valuable responsibility which has been bestowed upon women by the order of creation. There are a few points which are briey mentioned here with regard to this matter:

Fruit of Marriage

Although a man and a woman get married for a few reasons such as sexual motive, love, etc, having a child is not one of the main reasons for marriage.

But it is not long before the true motive of natural creation becomes apparent itself and the love for having a child grows in their hearts. The existence of a child is the fruit of the marital tree and a natural desire of men and women. A marriage without a child is like a fruitless tree. A child would strengthen the bonds of love between a couple. It serves as a drive to the man's working life and encourages the parents to care for their family.

Marriage is sometimes initially founded on the basis of lust, love making and instantaneous sexual interests. Such a foundation is false and not lasting and is always prone to destruction. The factor with which this foundation becomes strong, is having a child.

---

[139] Ibid, vol 103, p 258.

Lust and sexual drive soon subside. The only memory from days and nights of sexual desire would be the children, whose existence would be heart warming to the parents.

"Imam Sajjad (a.s) stated: 'One's happiness is in haying pious children from whom one can seek help.'"[140]

"The Prophet of Allah (S) stated: 'A pious child is a sweet-smelling plant from among the plants of Paradise.'"[141]

"The Prophet of Allah (S) also stated: ' Add to the numbers of your children, because I, on the Day of Judgment, will feel honored about the greatness of your numbers over the other Ummahs.'"[142]

How ignorant are those who, with various excuses, refuse to have children, and thus ght the principle of creation!

Educating a Child

The most sensitive responsibility of a mother is her duty to educate and train her children. Although both the parents should share this responsibility, it weighs more heavily on the shoulders of mothers.

This is because a mother is able to constantly protect and monitor her child. If mothers, through a correct program try to bring up their children, then a whole nation and even the world would undergo revolutionary changes.

Thus the progress or deterioration of a society is in the hands of women.

"The Prophet of Allah (S) stated: 'The Paradise is under the feet of mothers.'"[143]

---

[140] Wasa'il al-Shi'ah, vol 15, p 96

[141] Ibid, p 97

[142] Ibid, p 96

[143] Majm'a al-Zawa'id, vol 8, p 138

Part 1: The Duties of Women

Small children of today are the men and women of tomorrow. Whatever lessons they learn now, they will practice in future societies. If families improve, the society will progress, because societies are no more than a collection of families. Tomorrow's world will suffer with today's bad- tempered, stubborn, ignorant, cowardly, materialistic, nasty, careless, selsh and cruel children.

On the contrary, tomorrow's world will benet from today's children who are honest, well mannered, generous, brave, just, trustworthy, etc.

Therefore, parents in general and mothers in particular are responsible towards their societies. They can serve their society by bringing up pious children. On the other hand, carelessness about their responsibility will be questioned on the Day of Judgment.

"Imam Sajjad (a.s) stated: 'The right of your child is that you should know he is from you. Be it good or bad he is related to you. You are responsible for his upbringing, education and showing him the path to Allah and helping him to be obedient. You should treat him in such a way that if you behave well towards him, you will be sure of being rewarded and if you behave badly towards him, you will be sure of receiving punishment.'"[144]

Of course not all mothers are aware of the necessary skills of training a child and that is why they should set about learning them.

It is not within the scope of this book to present you with a detailed discussion on caring for one's child. Fortunately, there are many books, which have been written on this subject by learned writers and scholars. Women can buy these books and with the help of their own experience, they can educate their children and even become specialists in the eld of child-rearing. She can then become helpful to other mothers for their duties regarding their children.

Here one point should be mentioned. Many people make mistake

---

[144] Bihar al-Anwar, vol 74, p 6.

about the two phrases of 'education' and 'training', or think of them as having the same meaning. But one should know that teaching a child different subjects such as appropriate stories, poems, Qur'an, traditions of the Prophet (S), and the Imams (a.s) does not educate them. Such subjects are useful but a child should not only learn about honest persons, but he should be honest himself.

Thus, we must create such an atmosphere and living environment that the child would naturally become an honest and pious person. If a child grows up in an environment of honesty, truthfulness, bravery, discipline, cleanliness, kindness, love, freedom, justice, patience, trustworthiness, faithfulness, and sacrice, then he learns all of that.

On the other hand, a child who grows up in a place of corruption, deception, anger, hate, hypocrisy, lth, and disloyalty, would inevitably be affected by them. Such a child may learn many stories about good and pious people, but to no avail. Dishonest parents cannot, by teaching Qur'an and Hadith, bring up honest children. Dirty mother and father actually teach their child to be dirty. A child pays more attention to his parent's deeds and not so much to their words.

Therefore, those of us who are seriously thinking of bringing up honest and good children should correct their own behaviour rst. This is the only way to educate a child to be useful to himself and his society.

Nutrition and Hygiene

Another important duty of a housewife is feeding her children. Health or illness, beauty or ugliness, even good or bad temperedness, and cleverness of children are all related to the way they are fed.

Children have a different feeding pattern as compared with that of adults. They have different requirements at different ages and therefore mothers have to take this point into consideration when feeding their children.

"The best and the most nourishing food is milk. Milk contains all that is required for a healthy body. Thus for a baby there is nothing more suitable than the mother's milk. Since milk contains ingredients which are suitable for the baby's digestive system, therefore, there are not any problems in feeding a baby with mother's milk. Besides one does not need to boil it, pasteurize it, or sterilize it. One also need not to worry about its genuineness.

"Imam Ali (a.s) stated: 'There is no better and more copious food than mother's milk for a baby.'"[145]

"Dr A. H. Taba, the former Head of the Eastern Mediterranean Region of the World Health Organization said: 'One of the important factors, which makes a child susceptible to many illnesses is by depriving him or her of mother's milk which is the only life insurance of any person.'"[146]

Thus, mothers who feed their babies with their own milk must remember that all the necessary nutrition for their babies are contained within that milk.

But a nutritive milk is only possible if the mother is fed well, that is, the quality of her milk is related to the quality and quantity of her own food. The better her food, the better her milk would be. Mothers who feed their babies with their own milk can, through carelessness about their food, damage their own health as well as of their babies.

The fathers of small babies are also responsible to supply their wives with sufcient good quality food. Malnutrition is a serious problem for many people and one should not overlook it or else she must be prepared to pay for the treatment of illnesses caused by it.

You can obtain enough information on this subject from your doctor or related books. But as a general rule a nursing mother should consume all types of food from meat, fruit, dairy products to vegetables.

---

[145] Wasa'il al-Shi'ah, vol 15, p 175

[146] Ittela'at, 15th Farvardin, 1353 Solar Hijri

The important fact is that the mother's milk affects the baby's character and that is why "Imam Ali (a.s) stated: 'Do not choose foolish women to feed (your children) with their milk, because the milk makes their base qualities penetrated into the child.'"[147]

"Imam Baqir (a.s) stated: 'Choose noble women to feed (your children) with their milk, because the base qualities of milk are passed from the feeding woman to the child.'"[148]

You must feed your baby at denite intervals. Your child gets used to this regularity and helps him in being patient. It also helps him with regard to a healthy digestive system and stomach. On the other hand, if you feed the baby whenever he cries, then he will not learn to be disciplined. If he gets what he wants through crying, then he will pick up this attitude and use it even when he becomes an adult. He will not have the necessary patience when confronting hardships. He will either use force to achieve his own wishes or he will break down under difculties.

Do not think that to discipline a child is an impossible task. You must just be patient and have a suitable program for training him according to your standards. The child nutritive experts say that a baby must be fed with milk once every three to four hours.

Hold your child in your arms while feeding. By embracing the child feels your love and it would even affect his/her future personality. Do not feed the baby while lying down, because it has been seen that some mothers have fallen asleep while feeding their babies and as a result some babies have suffocated because their mother's breasts prevented them breathing.

If you do not have any milk yourself, you can use cow's milk. But since cow's milk is much denser than mother's milk, you must add some

---

[147] Wasa'il al-Shi'ah, vol 15, p 188

[148] Ibid, p 189.

water to it. You can also use pasteurized milk, which you should boil for twenty minutes or until it becomes safe for babies' consumption.

Do not feed the baby with hot or cold milk, but at the same temperature as the mother's milk.

After every feeding, you should boil the bottle and its nipple, and extra car must be taken during the hot seasons. Be careful not to use leftover or sour milk. It is better to measure the amount of milk for every feeding in order to make sure that your child is not getting too much or too little. In using powdered milk, you should consult a pediatrician. You must always use fresh powdered milk.

After the fourth month of the baby's birth you can start to feed him with fruit juice. From the age of six months, you can also start to feed him with solid foods and soups. You can feed him biscuits or sweet bread. Yogurt and cheese are also useful. You can gradually feed him with slight amounts of your own food.

Remember that your baby feels thirsty just as often as you do. Therefore, feed him with water as well, but do not try to make him drink tea or coffee. Fruits, vegetables, and soups are especially useful for growing infants.

Do not forget to be hygienic with regard to your baby's bedding, clothing, and nappies. Wash his face and hands often. Bathe him regularly, because infants are very susceptible towards dirt and germs and become ill easily.

You must vaccinate your children against such diseases as smallpox, chickenpox, whooping cough, infantile paralysis, scarlet fever, measles, and diphtheria. Vaccines are fortunately readily available in medical and health centers.

You can have healthy children by observing these codes of hygiene and cleanliness.

Part 2: The Duties of Men

The Guardian of the Family

Man and woman are the two basic pillars of a family, but since men are endowed with special qualities by the order of creation, and because their power of logic is stronger than women's, they are regarded as the guardians of their families.

The Almighty Allah regards men as the guardians of their families and states in the Holy Qur'an that:

> *"Men are the maintainers of women, because Allah has made some of them to excel others..." (The Holy Qur'an, 4:34)*

Therefore, men have a greater and more difcult responsibility in supporting their families.

It is the man who can, through his wisdom, support his family and prepare the grounds for their happiness and it is he who can turn the house into a paradise and his wife to act as an angel.

"The Prophet of Allah (S) stated: 'Man is the guardian of his family and every guardian has responsibilities towards those under his guardianship.'"[149]

A man, who is supporting his family, should know that a woman is also a human being like a man. She also has desires and the rights of freedom and life. Marrying a woman is not hiring a servant, but it is a selection of a partner and a friend who would be able to live with for the rest of one's life. Man has to care for her and her desires. Man is not the owner of his wife and in fact a woman has certain rights upon her husband.

Allah states in the Holy Qur'an:

> "...And women have rights similar to the rights of men in a just manner, and the men have a degree (of advantage) over them..." (The Holy Qur'an, 2:228).

Taking Care of your Wife

The secret to a family's prosperity is the way in which one takes care of one's wife, and this is, like the duty of a woman towards her husband which is regarded to be at the same level as Jihad, is also regarded as a man's best and most valuable act. But a married man must learn how to treat his wife in a way that she turns into an angel-like character.

For this, a man must nd out about his wife's behaviour and her desires. He must program his life according to her wishes and righteous requests. He can, through his own manners and attitude, inuence her in a way that interests her in both him and his house.

This is a subject which needs more explanation and detailed discussion will be presented later in this book.

---

[149] Mustadrak, vol 2, p 550.

Be Loving towards Her

A woman is a center of kindness and a being who is completely emotional. Her existence depends on compassion and affection. She longs to be loved by others and the more the better. She sacrices herself a great deal in order to seek popularity. This character is so strong in her that if she realizes nobody loves her, then she regards herself as a failure. She becomes disappointed in herself and feels dejected. Therefore, certainly one can claim that the secret of a successful man in a happy marital life is his expression of love towards his wife.

Dear Sir! Your wife before marrying you was enjoying her parents' love and kindness. Now that she has entered into marriage agreement with you and now that she has chosen to live with you for the rest of her life, she expects you to fulll her desires for love and affection. She expects you to show more love to her than she received from her parents and friends. She has trusted you extremely and that is why she has entrusted you with her existence.

The secret to a happy marriage is the expression of your affection to your wife.

If you want to conquer her heart, if you want to make her obedient with regard to your demands, if you want to strengthen your marriage, make her love you and remain faithful to you, or..., then you must always show your affection to her and express your love.

If you deprive your wife of kindness, then she would lose interest in her house, children and, above all, in you. Your house would always be in a messy condition. She would not be prepared to make efforts for a person who does not love her.

A house, in which there is no affection, resembles a burning hell, even though it may be very tidy and full of luxurious goods.

Your wife may become ill or have a nervous breakdown. She may seek popularity with others if she is not satised with you. She may grow so cold towards you and the house that she may even seek for a divorce.

You are responsible for all this because you have failed to keep her content. It is certainly true that some divorce procedures take place as a result of unkindliness.

Your attention is drawn to the following statistics. The psychological requirement of affection, the carelessness of husbands with regard to their wives' wishes and the overlooking of the importance of the mental status of women, have been responsible for many divorce cases.

"In the year 1969, out of a total of 10372 separations, 1203 women expressed the reason for their divorce as losing heart in life, feeling worthless, and the lack of care of their husband with regard to their wives' desires and emotional feelings."[150]

"A woman said in court that 'She was prepared to abandon her dowry and even pay her husband a sum of money to make him agree to a divorce. She said her husband was more interested in his parrots and that was why she did not want to live with him any longer."[151]

Family love and friendship is more precious than anything else and that is why Allah has regarded it as one of the signs of power and a great blessing which mankind has been endowed with, Holy Qur'an says:

> *"..And one of His signs is that He created mates for you from yourselves that you may nd rest in them and He put between you love and compassion; most surely there are signs in this for a people who reect." (The Holy Qur'an, 30:21)*

"Imam as-Sadiq (a.s) stated: 'Whoever is our friend, expresses his

---

[150] Ittela'at, 15th Azar, 1350 Solar Hijri.

[151] Ibid, 6th Bahman, 1350 Solar Hijri.

kindness to his spouse more.'"¹⁵²

"The Prophet of Allah (S) stated: 'The more one becomes faithful the more one expresses kindness to his spouse.'"¹⁵³

"Imam as-Sadiq (a.s) stated: 'One of the characteristics of the prophets of Allah is that they are all kind towards their wives.'"¹⁵⁴

"The Prophet of Allah (S) stated: 'The words of a man who tells his wife, 'I love you truly', should never leave her heart.'"¹⁵⁵

Love and affection must of course be genuine to appeal to another's heart, but even so loving for someone is not enough, as it is vital to express one's affection. By showing your feelings through your words and actions, the love you have shown will be returned to you and your hearts will strengthen their bonds of love.

Be frank and do not be discrete in expressing your love towards your wife. In her absence or presence, you should make compliments for her. Write to her while traveling and inform her that you miss her.

Occasionally buy something for her. Phone her when you are at work and ask how she is. One of the important things on a woman's mind is these kinds of expressions of love.

"Mrs… while shedding tears of grief said: 'I married my husband on an autumn night. We lived together in peace for a while. I regarded myself as the luckiest woman in this world. I lived in his little house for six years. I felt a hundred times happier when I found out that I was pregnant. When I informed my husband he wept tears of joy while embracing me in his arms. He cried so much that he nearly lost control over himself. He then went out and bought me a diamond necklace with his savings. He gave the necklace and said: 'I am giving this to

---

[152] Bihar al-Anwar, vol 103, p 227.

[153] Ibid, p 228.

[154] Ibid, p 236

[155] Shafi, vol 2, p 138.

the best woman that I have ever seen in the world'. But it was not long before he was killed in a driving accident.'"[156]

Respect Your Wife

A woman is proud of herself just the same as a man would be. She likes to be respected by others. She would get hurt if she were to be insulted or belittled. She feels good when respected and would hate those who try to degrade her.

Dear Sir! your wife surely expects you to respect her more than others. She has every right to expect her life partner and best friend to care for her.

She works for you and your children's comfort and thus expects you to value her efforts and to respect her. Honouring her would not belittle you but it would indeed go to prove your love and affection towards her. Therefore, respect her more than others and talk to her politely. Do not interrupt her or shout at her. Call her by respectful and virtuous names. Show your respect when she wants to sit down. When you enter the house, if she forgets to say 'Salam' (greetings), then you should say 'Salam' to her.

Say 'Good-bye' when leaving your house. Do not lose contact with her when travelling or away from home. Write to her. Show your respect for her when in gatherings. Seriously avoid all insults and humiliation. Do not abuse or even jokingly tease her. Do not think that because you are close to her she would not mind you making fun of her. On the contrary she will dislike such an attitude but may not express it.

"A dignied woman, around 35 years of age, says about her divorce request: 'It is twelve years that I have been married. My husband is a

---

[156] Ittela'at, 6th Bahman, 1348 Solar Hijri

good man and there are many characteristics of a good and amiable person in him. But he has never wanted to realize that I am his wife and the mother of both his children. He thinks he is a tting person for get togethers, but he performs his show by teasing and humiliating me. You cannot believe how much I have been hurt. My nerves have been affected so much that I have to go to a psychiatrist for treatment. I have talked to my husband about it many times. I have begged him not to treat me in this way. I have reminded him of my position as 'his wife' and my age and that it is not proper for him to joke with me in front of others so that they have a laugh or a good time. I feel embarrassed in front of everybody and because I have not ever been a witty person, I cannot compete with him. Since my demands are not being met by my husband, I prefer to separate from him. I know I will not be happy on my own, but I cannot live with a man who constantly degrades me.'"[157]

All women expect their husbands to respect them and all of them hate insults If some women keep silent before their husbands' humiliations, it is not the proof of their satisfaction.

If you respect your wife, she will do the same to you and thus your relationship will grow stronger. You would also earn more respect from others. If you maltreat her and she retaliates, it is again your fault and not hers.

Dear Sir! Marrying is not equal to getting a slave. You cannot treat a free person as a slave. Your wife has married you in order to live with you and to share her life with a man whom she loves. She expects the same things from you as you do from her. Therefore treat her in a manner in which you would like to be treated.

"Imam as-Sadiq (a.s), quoting his father, stated: 'Whoever marries, must respect his wife.'"[158]

---

[157] Ibid, 8th Esfand, 1350 Solar Hijri

[158] Bihar al-Anwar, vol 103, p 224.

"The Prophet of Allah (S) stated: 'Whoever respects a Muslim, Allah would pay him his own respect.'"[159]

"The Prophet of Allah (S) also stated: 'None would respect women except the magnanimous ones, and none would insult them except the ignoble ones.' In addition, the Prophet of Allah (S) stated: 'Whoever insults his family, would lose happiness in his life.'"[160]

Be Well-mannered

The world takes its path according to a regular pattern. Events happen and show themselves one after another. Our small existence in this vast universe is like a small particle which moves and impinges on other particles at every instant of time. The running of this world is not in our hands and the events of this world do not occur according to our will. From the moment that one sets foot outside his house in the morning until the time he returns home in the evening, one may be confronted with hundreds of unpleasant circumstances.

One comes across a great many difculties in the arena of life. You might be insulted by someone, have an unfriendly colleague, have to wait for the bus too long, have been accused of something at work, have lost some money, have been robbed, or have come across anyone of a number of similar events that could happen to anybody anywhere.

You might be so frustrated with the usual everyday events of your life that you resemble a time bomb which could explode any time.

Well you may think that you cannot blame other people or the world for your mishaps, so when you come home, you try to vent your anger out on your wife and children. You enter your house and it is as if 'Izrail (the angel of death) has arrived. The children disperse like little

---

[159] Ibid, vol 74, p 303.

[160] Mawa iz al-Adadiyyah, p 151

mice in front of you. God forbid that you should nd something to pick up fault. With! The food may be salty or salt less, your cup of tea may not be ready, the house may be untidy, or the children make a noise. And it gives you a good excuse to blow your top in your own house.

You then become furious and shout at every body, abuse them, hit the children, and so on. You will have then turned a house of affection and friendship into a burning hell in which you and the rest of your family would have to suffer.

If the children are able to run away from home into the streets, they would do so, and if they cannot do that, then they count the seconds until you leave the house.

It is patently obvious what an apathetic and horric atmosphere is dominant in families of this kind. There are always rows and arguments. Their house is always in a mess. The wife hates to see her husband's face.

How can a woman live happily with a grim and bad-tempered man?

Worse than all is the fate of children who are to grow up in such an environment. The parents' quarrels would certainly leave a scar on their sensitive souls and hearts. Children, who experience this kind of hardship, tend to become furious, aggressive, depressed, and pessimistic type of people in their adulthood. They become disheartened in their family and go astray. They might fall into the traps of corrupt people and turn to crimes of different kinds. They might even become so complexed and mentally disturbed that they might even endanger other lives and commit murder or even suicide.

The reader is recommended to conduct research into the backgrounds of criminals. Statistics and the daily news of criminal events all reect this fact.

Responsibilities of all these lie with the guardian of the family who has not been able to control his temper and who has mistreated his family. Such a person can never nd peace in this world and would be punished in the next.

Dear Sir! We are not in a position and cannot control the affairs of this world. Mishaps, hardships, and sorrowful events are all inseparable parts of this life. Everybody experiences difculties at different times. As a matter of fact, one can reach maturity through hardship. One must confront them with strength and must try to nd solutions to them.

Human beings have the ability to meet with hundreds of small and large difculties and not to give in under the strain of misfortune.

Worldly events are not the only reason for our being upset, but rather it is our nervous system which becomes affected by such events and causes us to experience discomfort. Therefore, if one could control himself when faced with the unhappy events of life, one would not become annoyed or angry.

Suppose that you have experienced an unpleasant event. This event is either an inseparable part of daily events with which we cannot interfere or that we cannot help. Or it might be an event in which we can thrust our own decision.

It is obvious that in the former case, our annoyance would not help in anyway. We would be wrong to become angry or bad-tempered. We must remember that we were not responsible for its occurrence and even try to welcome it with a smiling face. But if our bad experience is of the latter type, then we can seek a suitable solution for it.

If we do not lose heart when faced with hardships and try to control ourselves, we can, through prudence, overcome our difculties. In this way we would not resort to anger which may itself add to our problems. Therefore, a wise person is the one who is not affected by hardships.

We have the ability to overcome all difculties through patience and wisdom. Is it not a pity that we lose control over matters resulting from inevitable events of life?

Moreover, why should you blame your wife and children for your misfortunes?

Your wife is performing her share of duty. She has to take care of the house and the children. She has to do the washing, cooking, ironing, cleaning, etc. You should encourage her in the way you treat her.

Your children are also doing their own work. They too wait for their father to make themselves happy. Teach them the right things and encourage them in their studies.

Is it fair that you confront your family with a grim and angry face?

They expect you to fulll their righteous desires. They expect kindness from you and want you to talk to them gently and behave pleasantly.

They would hate you for ignoring their feelings and for turning the house into a dark place in which there is not a glimpse of happiness.

Do you know how much they could suffer from your unpleasant and harsh manners?

Even if you do not take your family very seriously, at least have mercy upon yourself. You can be sure that you would damage your own health by being bad-tempered.

How can you continue to work and how can you achieve anything successfully? Why should you turn your house into a hell?

Is it not better for you to always be happy and confront your problems with prudence and not anger?

Would you not prefer to believe that anger would not solve your problems, but rather it would add to them? Would you not agree that, while being at home, you should rest and regain your strength in order to nd a suitable solution to your problem with a clear mind? You should meet your family with a smile on your face. You should joke with them in a nice manner and try to create a happy atmosphere at home. You should eat and drink with them and take rest. In this way you and your family would enjoy life and you would overcome your problems easily.

That is why the holy religion of Islam regards good behaviour as a part of religion and a sign of the utmost level of faith.

"The Prophet of Allah (S) stated: 'Whoever is more well-behaved is more complete in his faith. The best among you (the people) is one who does good to his family.'"[161]

"The Prophet (S) also stated: 'There is no deed better than good behaviour.'"[162]

"Imam as-Sadiq (a.s) stated: 'Doing good to the people and behaving properly with them makes the cities populous and increases the age (of the citizens).'"[163]

"Imam as-Sadiq (a.s) also stated: ' An immoral person remains involved in torture and anguish.'"[164]

"Wise Luqman stated: ' A sagacious man must act like a child when with his family, and leave his manly behaviour for when out of his house.'"[165]

The Prophet of Allah (S) stated: 'There is no joy better than good behaviour.'"[166]

"The Prophet (S) also stated: 'Good behaviour is half the religion (of Islam).'"[167]

"It has been reported that when Sa'ad ibn Ma'adh, one of the great companions of the Holy Prophet (S) died, the Holy Prophet (S) took part in his funeral with bare feet, as if he had lost someone from among his own family.

The Prophet (S) placed the dead body in the grave with his pious hands and then covered it. The mother of Sa'ad who was observing

---

[161] Bihar al-Anwar, vol 103, p 226.

[162] Shafi, vol 1, p 166.

[163] Ibid

[164] Ibid, p 176.

[165] Mahajjat al-Bayda, vol 2, p 54

[166] Bihar al-Anwar, vol 71, p 389.

[167] Ibid, p 385.

the Holy Prophet's (SA) respect for her son, addressed Sa'ad and said: 'O Sa'ad! enjoy Paradise.' The Prophet of Allah (S) told her: 'O mother of Sa'ad, do not say that, because Sa'ad has just experienced Daghtat al-Qabr[168] (torment by way of compression in the grave etc). Later, when the Prophet (S) was asked about the reason for Sa'ad's Daghat al-Qabr, the Prophet (S) replied: 'it was because he (Sa'ad) was maltreating his family.'"[169]

Complaining Unnecessarily

The problems of life are many. There is not anyone who is completely happy with his situation. But some people are more patient with their hardships than others, they try to record them in their memories and do not mention them except when there is reason or revealing them.

On the other hand, there are people who are so weak that they cannot keep any problem to themselves.

They are so used to making complaints that upon meeting others, they start complaining. Wherever they, go and whenever they are in a gathering, they moan about the everyday events which have effected their lives it is as if they haven sent on a mission by Satan himself, to spoil the happiness of others. That is why most friends and relatives do not want to be bothered with these and try to keep away from them as much as possible.

But one must feel sorry for their wives and children who have to cope with them. Because no one else is prepared to listen to their moaning, these men vent their problems before their families.

They sometimes complain about their expenses, the taxis, their

---

[168] Daghtat al-Qabr: 'Compression in the grave' which is a kind of torment for the deceased person against his sins.

[169] Ibid, vol 73, p 298

friends, and sometimes they moan about their colleagues, their businesses, diseases, doctors, and so on.

These men are very pessimistic and, do not see any good in this world. They suffer themselves as well as make and especially their families, suffer too.

Dear Sir! What is the point of making complaints all the time? What do you achieve by moaning? Why should your family suffer if you are angry with the taxi driver? Why do you blame your wife if your business is not brisk?

Do not forget that your attitude would repel your family from you. They will become disappointed in you and disheartened with the house. They might even run away from home and might fall into the trap of corruption and crime. The least is that it leaves a mental scar on them.

Is it not better not to spoil your family's happiness?

When returning home, try to forget your problems. Be happy with your family. Eat with them. Have a laugh and enjoy their company.

Islam has also regarded patience and refusing to make complaints as good behaviour and has even allocated a reward for it.

"Imam Ali (a.s.) stated: 'When hardship falls upon a Muslim, he should not make complaints about Allah to other people, but that he should take the problems to Allah who possesses the key to all problems.'"[170]

"Imam Ali (a.s) also stated: 'It is written in the Tawrah: whoever makes a complaint about a hardship

which has befallen him, is in fact complaining about Allah.'"[171]

"The Prophet (S) of Islam stated: 'Whoever experiences hardship with his health and does not make complaints (about it) to people, then

---

[170] Bihar al-Anwar, vol 72, p 326

[171] Ibid, p196.

it is incumbent on Allah to forgive all his sins.'"[172]

Picking up Quarrels

Some men are constantly seeking excuses to pick up fault with everything. They moan at every trivial matter: "Why is this table dirty? Why is the lunch not ready? Why is that vase here? Have I not said before that ashtrays should not be on the oor?" etc...

Some men take this attitude so far that it causes rows and quarrels within their family, and sometimes a family break-down as a result of their behaviour.

Of course we are not saying that men do not have the right to tell their wives what to do and what not to do. In the rst part of this book, women were recommended to acknowledge this right. There we stated that women should not show stubbornness towards their husbands' suggestions regarding household affairs. However, men should keep their logic and wisdom. They are their families' guardians and as such they should act properly.

If a man wants to successfully participate in the affairs of the house then he should do so in a calculated manner.

As a matter of fact, since a man does not have enough time to participate in all the matters regarding his house and because he lacks the necessary expertise in this connection, then it is to his advantage to leave the housework to his wife. A man should leave his wife at liberty with regard to running the house.

Men can, however, under the pretext of consultation, not forcefully, remind their wives about certain points. Once a wise woman nds out her husband's wishes about any matter, she would try to conform with them. Therefore, a man and a woman who care for each other and their

---

[172] Majm'a al-Zawaid, vol 3, p 331.

family, can through talking together in a kind manner, reach many agreements on all matters. In this way, most women are prepared to conform with their husbands' occasional demands.

But if his participation takes the form of picking up fault and constant moaning, then the housewife gets used to them and consequently this attitude becomes a usual affair from which nothing useful would result.

A woman with a moaning husband would not take him seriously. She may even ignore his proper and important points of concern. She would reason for herself "Why should I waste my energy, if my husband is not ever satised with my work?"

Not only would she ignore her husband's criticism, but might even take retaliatory measures.

This is when their house turns into a battleeld. Constant criticism of each other would then prepare the ground for separation and thus a family unit breaks down. In this scenario the woman is not to be blamed because even a wise and patient wife would run out of patience as a result of continuously humiliating attitude of her husband.

"A man called the police station and claimed that his wife had left his house two months ago and that she was living with her parents. After further enquiries, this man's wife said:

'My husband does not like my style of housekeeping. He constantly criticizes me on my cooking and running the affairs of house. Therefore, I have left him to nd peace somewhere else.'"[173]

Men should remember that housework is an area for their wives to perform their duties. It is wrong to deprive them of their rights or to turn them into puppets. It is wiser to leave them to run the house the way they like.

As a result, your wife does her job enthusiastically, you would remain happy and your house would be a home for a happy family.

---

[173] Ittela'at, 16th Urdibahisht, 1351 Solar Hijri

Appease Her and Sympathize with Her

A woman also, similar to a man, undergoes emotional changes. She experiences happiness, anger, sorrow, etc. She becomes tired from housework and may become annoyed with the children. Others may upset her by their criticisms. She might become involved in competing with others. In short, a woman confronts many problems of which some may affect her so much so that she might become desperate to such an extent so as to react unkindly towards trivial matters.

This is especially the case for women, because they are very sensitive and would react more critically towards unpleasant events as compared to men.

Women, who experience hardship, need appeasing. Men must comfort them because they are their partners and the ones who are trusted by their wives.

Dear Sir! When you nd your wife in a state of distress and anger, then try to understand her situation. If you enter your house and she does not salute you, you say 'salam' to her. This would not belittle you.

Talk to her with a smiling face. Avoid-grimness. Help her in the housework. Be careful not to offend her in any way. Do not tease her. If she is not in a mood to talk, then leave her alone. Do not say: 'What is wrong with you?'

If she feels like talking, listen to her and sympathize with her. Pretend you are more concerned with her problem than herself. Let her reveal her grievances for you. Then like a kind father or a sympathetic husband try to help her nd a solution to her problem. Encourage her to be patient. Through wisdom and logic make her regard her problems as trivial. Strengthen her character and assist her in overcoming the cause of her annoyance.

Be patient and treat her according to your logic. She would certainly nd your help useful and life will soon get back to normal for both of you.

On the contrary, your wrong approach would cause more distress for her. You would also suffer and it might even turn into a major row from which, both of you would suffer.

Do not pick up Faults

There is no one in this world who has all the qualities and free from all the faults. Some people may be too fat or too thin. Their mouth may be too big, have large noses or big teeth. Others may be dirty, impolite, shy, cheeky, depressed, bad-tempered, jealous, lazy or selsh. Some women may not be good cooks or talented hostesses. Some people may eat too much or spend lavishly. In brief, everyone is imperfect and no one in this world can be regarded as a perfect being.

Men usually, before marriage, imagine their ideal woman to be devoid of all faults. They ignore this fact that there is no angel-like gure in our universe. These men, once married, nd their ideal wives not to be perfect and thus start to point out their faults. They might even regard their marriages as failures and call themselves 'unlucky'.

These men are always moaning and do not even spare the trivial faults of their wives.

Some men exaggerate the faults so much that they always appear before them like high mountains. They occasionally mention these faults to their wives and humiliate them. They might even mention them before friends and relatives.

As a result, the foundation of their marital life starts trembling. The woman becomes depressed and loses interest in her husband and family. She would think it illogical to work in the house of someone who criticizes her. She might even take retaliatory measures.

The man says to his wife: "What a big and ugly nose you have!?" And the woman replies: "It is not as bad as your ugly face and deformed gure!" The man would then say: "Your feet smell foul!" And the woman replies: "Shut up your big mouth!" etc.

A continuation of this conversation opens the door for criticisms and turns the house into a battleeld in which the couple insults and degrades each other.

If they live like this, they would not enjoy their lives ever again, because a house devoid of family love and sincerity, is not a place of comfort.

Moreover, a man who regards himself as unlucky and his marriage as a failure, and a woman who is constantly being humiliated, are both prone to mental disorders and other illnesses.

If the magnitude of their row becomes larger then there is always the danger of divorce and separation. A divorce is not very helpful to either party especially if there are children in the family.

Society does not have much respect for a divorcee. Moreover, a divorce would inict economic losses on a man, which are not easily repairable. This is especially true if he wants to re-marry, since he would also have to spend money on his second marriage. Furthermore, it is not at all clear that a divorcee is able to nd another woman who would live up to his expectations.

Re-marriage would not be easy for him because of his past record. Even if he nds another woman, she would denitely possess certain faults also. She may even turn out to be worse than his rst wife. He would then have to cope with her. This is because some men are too proud to confess their shortcomings. It is rare to nd a man who is fully satised with his second marriage. It has even been seen that some men return to their rst wives.

Dear Sir! Why should you look at your wife with a view of nding her faults and why do you place so much importance on her trivial defects? Why do you magnify her deciencies so much so that it causes suffering for you and your family? Have you ever seen a perfect woman? Are you perfect yourself? What are trivial deciencies worth that you endanger your marriage for their sake?

Be certain that if you look at your wife with a logical and fair view, you would see many good points about her. You look and see that her merits would outweigh her deciencies.

Islam regards this attitude as harmful and distasteful and thus forbids all from nding other people's faults.

"The Prophet of Allah (S) stated: 'O you who express to be Muslims by tongue only but faith has not entered your hearts! Do not speak ill of Muslims and do not set out to nd their faults (because) whoever picks up fault with others, would be criticized by Allah and even if such a person is at his house, he would be disgraced.'"[174]

Do not Pay Attention to Slanderous Talk of the Critics

Some people are in the habit of uttering slander about others. This distasteful behaviour creates enmity among friends and relatives and can break families. It has even been responsible for murder. There are various reasons for such behaviour, like jealousy, anger, vengeance and hostility.

Some people resort to defamatory words in order to satisfy their own ego, to attract others' attention towards themselves, or to pretend to be sympathetic with someone else. But it is rarely a case that slanderous statements are based on good intentions.

Therefore, a wise and clever man should ignore such statements. He must always analyze the statements of the speaker in order not to be deceived or inuenced by his evil insinuations.

One of the points for men to remember is that generally their mothers, sisters and brothers, despite their apparent friendship, do not

---

[174] Shafi, vol 1, p 206

enjoy a good relationship with their wives.

The reason is that a man, before marriage, spends years with his parents where he does not have much independence. His parents, who have worked hard to bring him up, expect him to be helpful to them in their old age.

Even after they marry their son off and apparently give him independence, they expect him to conform to their own will and wishes. They like their son to pay more attention to them than to his wife. But the reality is that when a man starts a marital life, he makes a great deal of effort for his new family, wife, and independence. He directs his love towards his wife and works hard in this connection. The more he steps in this direction, the farther he goes away from his parents.

Thus his mother and sister(s) specially feel offended. They regard their new bride as a threat who would be taking their young boy away from them. They might even blame their bride for separating their boy from his family.

Mothers may sometimes think that the best way of confronting this danger is by implementing ways of lessening their sons' affection towards their wives. A mother of this kind would then start to point out her daughter-in-law's deciencies, spread lies about her, speak defamatory words about her, conspire against her, etc.

If a man is simple or naive, he might even be inuenced by his mother's defamatory statements. He would then become a tool in the hands of his family after which he would lose interest in his wife. Under his parents' inuence, the man would start to moan and pick up faults with his wife. He would criticize her on any possible occasion.

As a result, the family house could turn into a cold and dull place.

Instigations of men by their mothers and sisters could lead to rows and even ghts between a man and his wife. A wife in this condition might resort to drastic measures such as committing suicide.

"A newly married woman swallowed pins at the end of her rst week of marriage. After an operation on her to remove the pins from her stomach, she said in the hospital: 'About a week ago, I was married. The day I entered the house of my husband, I felt as lucky as other married women. But after only a few days, my husband and his sister started criticizing me. Their attitude made life very difcult for me. Finally I decided to kill myself and swallowed a few pins.'"[175]

"A woman who was frustrated with the criticisms of her husband's brothers, set re on herself and died of severe burns."[176]

"A newly married woman became so frustrated with the bad attitude of her mother-in-law that she burnt herself to death."[177]

Therefore, criticisms, bad attitudes, and defamatory words of mothers, sisters and brothers-in-law can be very harmful and thus a man must be aware of their nuisance. Of course it is not possible to stop people from talking but it is possible to neutralize their talks.

A man must be aware that criticisms about his wife by his mother, sister, etc are not meant to be sympathetic and out of good intentions, but the main reasons are jealousy, enmity, selshness, etc.

He must remember that because his wife draws much of his attention towards herself, his family envies her and regards her as a usurper of their young man. Therefore, they resort to ways of preventing their love to grow.

Dear Sirs! In brief, mothers, sisters, and brothers of this kind are not bothered with your happiness, but rather they are concerned with their own interests. If they were concerned with your happiness, they would have done something different.

It is very strange that parents make a great deal of compliments of a woman who wants to marry their son, but once their son marries that

---

[175] Ittela'at, 25th Aban, 1348 Solar Hijri

[176] Ibid, 14th Murdad, 1349 Solar Hijri

[177] Ibid, 13th Urdibahisht, 1349 Solar Hijri.

woman, the parents turn completely the opposite way.

Dear Sir! Do not be deceived. Those deciencies that your family set forth for your wife are not relevant; and even if they are not trivial, then remember that nobody is perfect.

Anyway, are your sister, mother or others who criticize your wife, themselves perfect beings?

Paying attention to their slanderous statements would only adversely affect your family life. You might even end up with a divorce as a result of which you would suffer mentally and economically.

A re-marriage would not be easy. Even if you nd another woman to marry, it is not at all obvious that she is any better than your former wife. How do you make sure that your family would not treat her as badly as they did with your former wife?

So it is better for you to tell your mother, sister and others right now that your wife suits you and that you love her. You must declare to them that they should stop criticizing your wife or else your wife or else you would cut off your relationship with them. Once they feel your rm attitude, they would stop their instigative attitude and you may nd peace with your wife.

But unfortunately, some mothers and sisters do not give up easily and resort to malicious accusations such as adultery. The problem becomes so serious that a man might, based on his mother's statements, divorce his wife or even kill her.

"A young couple took their divorce application to a court in Tabriz. The man said in the court: 'My wife writes love-letters to my brother who lives in Isfahan. I found a few of her letters last night'. His wife while crying, said: 'My mother and sister-in-law do not like me and constantly disturb me. But now that their mischievous deeds have not affected my husband, they have forged some love-letters and have placed them in my wardrobe in order to instigate him to divorce me'. The court reconciled the couple with each other and advised the man to tell his mother and sister to stop their malicious acts towards their bride."[178]

"A thirty-four year old woman emptied a can of kerosene on herself and set herself on re. Neighbours soon put the re out and took her to the hospital. She said in the hospital: 'I live with my husband and his mother. She constantly picks up fault with me. She raises excuses and is very furious in nature. She does not miss an opportunity to create a row between me and my husband. Yesterday I went for shopping and accidentally met one of my old school friends. We talked a while and then I returned home. My mother-in-law started questioning me as to why I was late? I explained but she was not satised. She said that I was lying and that I was having an affair with the butcher in our street. I got furious and felt so frustrated that I decided to kill myself."[179]

Therefore, a man should always be aware of such allegations which could have disastrous ends. He should make enquiries about them patiently and not jump to conclusions blindly.

Of course one's parents work hard and suffer a great deal in bringing up their children and thus make them become the centre of all their hopes. They expect him to be a helping hand for them in their old age and their expectations are just that. So it is not fair that when one gains independency, he should forget about his duties towards his parents. He should attend to their rightful wishes even after he is married. He must maintain their respect and be humble before them. He is duty-bound to help them money wise if they ever needed it. He should not cut off his relationship with them and must invite them to his house. He must demand his wife and children to show their respect for them. He must make his wife understand that if she would respect his parents, they would not feel the necessity of annoying her

---

[178] Ibid, 3rd Esfand, 1350 Solar Hijri.

[179] Kayhan, 25th Farvardin, 1352 Solar Hijri.

and would even be proud of her and support her.

Finally women are reminded that they have no right to expect their husbands to abandon their parents. This expectation is neither possible nor fair. A wise woman can treat her in-laws in such a way that they would regard her as an important member of their own family. This is only possible if she respects them, seeks advice from them, helps them, etc.

This discussion was presented in detail in the rst part to which you can refer to for more information.

Overlook Her Mistakes

Other than the Infallible ones (whom Allah has vowed to keep away from sins), no human being is perfect and all of us make many mistakes. Of course this is true for both men and women.

In the case of women, she may make mistakes by being impolite to her husband, do something against his wish, be harsh to him, or inict an economic loss on him by being careless, etc.

Of course it is true that a couple should keep each other satised and should seriously avoid annoying each other; however, it rarely happens that one or both parties do not deviate from this line.

Some men think that they should be strict about their wives' mistakes as they believe this to be the way to prevent the repetition of the same mistake again.

However, experience often shows exactly the reverse to be the case. A woman, whose husband is strict with her, may be able to cope with his strictness for a while, but would eventually decide to react against it as a result of frustration. She gradually gets used to his attitude until she becomes indifferent towards it.

A husband who would not practice forgiveness with regard to his wife's mistakes, is practically encouraging her to become impudent and disobedient. He might wish to continue this attitude where he will surely have many rows with his wife. They both would have to live in a state of bitterness for the rest of their lives.

Or he might choose to leave his wife alone and not concern himself with her as much. In this case his wife, who feels she has won a ght, becomes indifferent to her husband's will and wishes. It might reach a point that even when she commits major mistakes deliberately, he keeps silent. Their marriage then loses its warmth and they might resort to divorce.

Remember that a divorce is harmful to both parties because starting a new life is not so easy. Happiness cannot be guaranteed after divorce. Therefore, strictness is not always useful and often results in undesired events which one can read about in the media. The best way is to remain moderate and to act logically. Forgive all the trivial and non-deliberate mistakes of your wife. There is no need to shout at someone for a mistake which has happened erroneously. Of course, one can always advise others in order to help them not to repeat their mistakes.

People make many mistakes out of ignorance, so it is better to advise them patiently to correct their incorrect deeds or opinions.

Therefore, your wife cannot be forced into correcting her mistakes, but instead you should explain her mistake and its harmful effects logically so that she could choose herself not to repeat that action again. Thus not only your mutual respect remains as before, but it would also prevent the repetition of the same mistakes.

It is wise for a man to logically stop his wife from making mistakes, but if she persistently makes errors, then again he should forgive and overlook them. It is wrong for him to set about punishing her or trying to prove her guilt in order to make her apologetic. This is because women are stubborn by nature, and improper strictness makes them react more severely than before. This might be followed by unpleasant or even horric events, such as divorce or murder.

Islam has recognized this sensitive point where men have been made responsible for their women.

"Imam Ali (a.s) stated: 'Cope with women under all circumstances and speak to them well; (and by doing so) it may make their actions correct.'"[180]

"Imam Sajjad (a.s) stated: 'It is a right of (your) wife that you treat her kindly, because she is under your surety, and you should feed and dress her, and forgive her ignorant deeds.'"[181]

"Imam as-Sadiq (a.s) was asked: 'What rights a woman has on her husband, for which, if he acted accordingly, would be regarded as a good-doer?' The Imam replied: 'He must provide her with food and clothes and he should forgive her mistakes committed unknowingly.'"[182]

"Imam as-Sadiq (a.s) also stated: 'Whoever punishes those who are subordinate to him, should not expect to be honoured or to attain high ranks.'"[183]

One of the causes of rows among men and women is because men mothers-in-law butt into their family affairs.

A mother, before marrying her daughter off to a man, imagines her son-in-law to be perfect and approves for her daughter one who could make her happy. She would respect him and would treat him kindly in the hope of being able to correct his trivial faults at a later stage.

Sometimes she nds her son-in-law conforms to her expectation, and sometimes he does not. In the latter case, she intends to shape him until he can be accepted by her and for this she uses every possible means such as her own and others' experiences, and starts to plan her

---

[180] Bihar al-Anwar, vol 103, p 223.

[181] Ibid, vol 74, p 5.

[182] Shafi, vol 2. p 139

[183] Bihar al-Anwar, vol 75, p 272

approach.

She sometimes pretends to be sympathetic and sometimes strict. She might act as a guide and a supervisor, or might complain. However, the best option is to achieve her goal by inuencing her daughter by making her not conform to her husband.

She uses her daughter and thus orders her to act differently at various times. Consequently, the man nds his wife to be critical of him one day and begging him to do something the next day.

An inexperienced woman would think that her mother would be sympathetic to her marriage and would conform to her advice!

Thus if her husband still does not conform to his mother-in-law's ideal man, rows may break out between the couple which could result in divorce and even murder. That is why most men are not on good terms with their mothers-in-law. They blame them for their wives' disobedience and believe that their mothers put words in their daughters' mouths.

It would not be a bad idea if one learns about complaints of a few sons-in-law.

"Mr. M. Javad writes: 'My mother-in-law is a demon, a dragon, a two-headed serpent. May God save the wolves from her. She has made my life so bitter that I am going crazy and feel like running away to the mountains and deserts… It is not only me who is fed up with this situation. This is a general case and I think ninety-ve percent of men are affected by them and the other ve percent probably do not have a mother-in-law'.

Mr. F. Muhammad writes: 'My mother-in-law is always butting into my life. She causes our annoyance for no good reason. She is always speaking defamatory words about my family. Whenever I buy anything for my wife, she (the mother-in-law) starts picking up fault with it. She criticizes its colour, or model and tries to prove it worthless to my wife.'Mr. K Parviz writes: 'My mother-in-law has treated me in such a way that I have almost divorced my wife three times. She stings like a scorpion. She teaches my wife to be rude to me, to leave the housework, or to expect the impossible from me. Whenever she comes to us, our house turns into hell. I truly hate the sight of her.'"[184]

Most men try to counter their mothers-in-law's inuences on their wives by restricting their relationship with them. They stop their wives from going to their parents' houses. In brief, men do not get along with their mothers-in- law and show their dislike for them by all possible means.

However, this approach, although usual, is not logical and wise. This is because a mother daughter relationship is very strong and is a natural bond which cannot be broken easily.

How can a man expect his wife to abandon her parents who have spent years trying to bring her up?

This expectation is not practical and even if it happens, it would not be permanent, as any unnatural act is temporary.

Besides if a woman feels that her husband is against her parents, she might take up a similar stance with regard to his family. She may become disobedient, disrespectful, etc.

Moreover, this attitude of the man gives an excuse to his mother-in-law to interfere more severely in their marriage. In brief this approach could have a negative result and might lead to divorce.

Anyway why should a man, who can benet from associating with his in-laws, resort to such measures which could harm him and his family?

"Indian police authorities reported that in the year 1971, the main reason for a total of 146 cases of suicide in New Delhi was due to an unfavorable relationship between men and their mothers-in-law."[185]

"A man, who was frustrated with his mother-in-law because of her

---

[184] Ittela'at, Weekly. no 1646

[185] Kayhan, 15th Farvardin, 1352 Solar Hijri.

obtrusions, threw her out of a taxi."[186]

"A man broke his mother-in-law's skull with a hammer. His brother-in-law then became furious with him and after wounding him with a knife, escaped."[187]

"Mr…, who was angry with his mother-in-law, poured the contents of a hot stew over her head. She screamed and fainted on the oor. She was taken to hospital and after recovery said her daughter had informed her husband that she wanted a divorce and could not live with him any longer."[188]

"A man who was fed up with his mother-in-law committed suicide."[189] Here it is perhaps worth mentioning two points:

1. Obviously a mother-in-law, not only is not an enemy to her son-in-law, but it is natural for her to like him as is evident at the beginning of a marriage. Besides she nds herself close to him because of the interest that she has in her daughter's happiness. Therefore, when a mother-in-law interferes in her daughter's life, it cannot be meant to be anything but with good intentions. She means to be sympathetic, but sometimes out of ignorance, she takes the wrong steps or makes harmful suggestions. Thus one should not be too critical of such women.
2. A mother and child relationship is a natural bond which cannot be easily broken, and whoever makes efforts in this direction. Would surely fail. Such effort is contrary to the laws of nature and cannot be justied in any way.

---

[186] Ittela'at, 13th Urdibahisht, 1349 Solar Hijri

[187] Kayhan, 4th Esfand, 1350 Solar Hijri

[188] Ittela'at, 14th Esfand, 1350 Solar Hijri.

[189] Ibid, 12th Urdibahisht, 1349 Solar Hijri

Just as a man is interested in his parents, so is a woman. Consequently it is best to have a kind of relationship with one's in-laws that is benecial to both parties. This is only possible if one exercises respect and kindness. A man can, through wisdom, respect, obedience, etc have a good relationship with his mother-and father-in-law.

He should show his love for their daughter. He should not criticize her in front of them. He should seek advice and spiritual help from them. In the event of their suggesting or doing something wrong. He should kindly and logically point out to them that they are not right. He should not speak harshly to them.

A married man should regard a good relationship with his in-laws, as his duty and a secret to a successful marriage. As a result many family problems are prevented while many more can be resolved.

In brief, it is not always the mother-in-law who is guilty but men should be wise enough to be friend them.

There are many men who enjoy a good relationship with their mothers-in-law.

"Mr. Manuchehr writes: 'My mother-in-law is an angel or even better. I love her more than my own mother, because she is kind and understanding. She always helps us with our problems. Her existence is a guarantee of my family's happiness and prosperity.'"[190]

Even if a man has a mother-in-law who is stubborn, ignorant and impossible to reconcile with, he should not treat her harshly. This kind of women may make one's life difcult, but it is always better to react softly towards their improper behaviour. This is because, by treating them kindly, one could minimize the danger to one's marriage.

Meanwhile, the man should get closer to his wife and should make her trust him. He must discuss her mother's wrong deeds with her, and logically prove to her, their undesirable consequences.

---

[190] Ibid, Weekly, no 1646.

If a man is able to create a deep understanding with his wife, then many problems, including the one with his mother-in-law would be solved.

So do not forget good manners, be wise and treat your family kindly in order to have a successful marriage.

"Imam Ali (a.s) stated: 'Developing friendship is half of wisdom.'"[191]

"Imam 'Ali (a.s) also stated: 'Associating with people and treating them with good manners would prevent one from committing bad deeds and mischievous acts.'"[192]

"Imam Ali (a.s.) stated: 'Associate with each other and do good. Keep away from sulking and separation.'"[193]

Be Attentive

Woman is an emotional being whose emotions are dominant over her logic. She is more naive and sensitive than a man. She can be deceived more easily and has less control over her emotional desires. She cannot decide wisely once she is upset. She can be amused or made upset with little effort. Thus if the man has supervision over the behaviour and actions of his wife, most of the possible risks would be averted.

This is why the holy religion of Islam appoints men to act as guardians of their families and makes them responsible for their family affairs. Allah states in the Holy Qur'an:

> *"Men are the maintainers of women because Allah has made some of them to excel others and because they spend out of their property; the good women are therefore obedient,*

---

[191] Bihar al-Anwar, vol 74, p 168.

[192] Ibid.

[193] Ibid, p 400

guarding the unseen as Allah has guarded." (The Holy Qur'an, 4:34)

Therefore a man, who is regarded as the protector of his family, should not practise carelessness with regard to his wife's deeds, He must always supervise her affairs and monitor her actions, He must see to it that she does not deviate or associate with the wrong kind of people. He must logically explain to her the harms of keeping bad company. He must not allow her to leave the house with indecent clothing or which arouse sexual feelings, He must not permit her to participate in corrupt activities or to attend unworthy gatherings.

It is a fact that if a woman is left alone in her deeds and associations, she would possibly fall into the traps of evil-minded people who live in a corrupt life.

Men are recommended to take a look at the number of women who, as a result of their husbands' negligence, have fallen prey to corruption; there are many women who have been deceived at night parties. Many families have broken down and many children have lost their families as a result of such get-togethers.

A man who allows his wife to leave the house with indecent clothes, permits her to befriend all kinds of people, and does not stop her from attending corrupt gatherings, is in fact committing the greatest perdious act to himself, his wife, and children.

This attitude would lead his wife towards hundreds of danger zones from which she cannot easily escape. Petrol is inammable and re can burn it, thus it is foolish to think that leaving petrol next to re would not set it ablaze.

How ignorant and simple minded are those men who allow their wives or daughters, by being indecently dressed, to expose themselves in the streets, while at the same time disliking the attention or notice given to them by the youth.

Wrong freedoms of this kind have grave consequences. If a woman is successful in taming her husband with regard to her unlawful desires, she would then increase the extension of her wishes up to a level where she would act independently of her husband altogether. This will result in mischievous events in the family.

"That is why the Prophet (S) of Islam stated: 'A man is the guardian of his family and any guardian is responsible to his subordinates to take care of their needs.'"[194]

"The Prophet (S) also stated: 'Order women to do good deeds before they make you commit wrong ones.'"[195]

"In addition the Prophet (S) stated: 'Whoever obeys his wife, Allah would cast him into the re on his face.'"

"The Prophet (S) was asked: 'What sort of obedience is meant here'? The Prophet of Allah (S) replied: 'It is when the husband permits a woman who asks her husband to allow her to go to the public bath, weddings, celebrations, and condolence gatherings while wearing delicate and thin clothes.'"[196]

"Imam as-Sadiq (a.s) stated: 'The bliss of a man is that he becomes supervisor and guardian of his family.'"[197]

"The Prophet (S) of Islam stated: ' Any man who permits his wife, who has adorned herself, to leave the house, is a mean-spirited person, and whoever calls him as such, would not have committed any sin.

And any woman whose husband permits her to leave the house adorned and perfumed, with each step that she takes, Allah would build a house for her husband in hell.'"[198]

---

[194] Mustadrak, vol 2, p 550

[195] Bihar al-Anwar, vol 103, p 227

[196] Ibid, p 228.

[197] Wasa.il al-Shi'ah, vol 15, p 251

[198] Bihar al-Anwar, vol 103, p 249.

Finally, I remind you of two points:

1. It is correct that a man should be watchful of his wife but this should be done carefully and wisely. He must not resort to anger or violence. He must not make his wife feel that she is being ordered about or else she would react unpleasantly. The best way is, for the man, to be kind and understanding. He must act like a sympathetic partner and explain to his wife about the harms of wrong deeds. She must be made to choose the right path herself with enthusiasm and eagerness.
2. A man should be moderate, that is, he should neither be too strict and fussy, nor should be care- free. A woman, like a man, needs freedom and should be at liberty in her rightful associations. She must be free to communicate with her parents, brothers, and sisters and must be allowed to keep the appropriate type of company.

In brief, there are exceptional cases where a woman should be deprived of her desires. But even in such cases one should not step beyond the limits and become too strict. Too much strictness is harmful. It destroys a friendly atmosphere and causes annoyance. A woman might react severely as a result of her husband's strictness. She might even ask for a divorce.

"A young woman, Mrs... said to the reporter in the court: 'I got married with Mr ...ve years ago. We have a son and a daughter now. At times my husband has been treating everybody in a cynical manner. He does not allow me to associate with anybody. He even locks the doors for us when he leaves the house. We are prisoners in his house. I can't even go to my parents any more. My family-members do not come to us either, because of him. I do not know what to do! On the one hand I cannot live with him, and on the other, I am worried about my children's future. So, I decided to take my case to this court; perhaps they can pass some judgment.'"[199]

Men such as this woman's husband are, unfortunately, so strict and abnormal that their wives, despite their wish to live together, apply for divorce. Their wives become so annoyed with them that, despite having children, they are prepared to separate from them.

Why should a man forbid his wife from associating with her near-relatives? Does he not know that too much strictness prepares the grounds for some women to deviate from modesty? Has he not heard of or seen any shattered families as a result of such behaviour?

Even if one's wife copes with one's strictness, there would be a lack of warm family atmosphere in the house. How can one expect an imprisoned housewife to be kind to her husband and children or to eagerly pursue the housework?

The Disciplinary Rights of the Husband

Although a husband and wife, who form a joint family life, share and cooperate in running the affairs of their house, they may have different opinions over certain matters. A man might feel that it should be he who should decide about family affairs, with his wife's indisputable agreement. At the same time his wife may object to her role as the obedient party.

Arguments and rows may then start because both parties attempt to establish their authority over the other. The best solution to such a problem is that both should try to refrain from acting as superior to the other, and try to resolve their problems through dialogue and deep understanding. This would only be feasible if both of them stop being stubborn.

---

[199] Ittela'at, 14th Farvardin, 1351 Solar Hijri

Some men order their wives to do many things and if are confronted with resistance, they think it right to become annoyed, to punish or even to physically hurt their wives. This approach is not correct at all. The men of the 'Age of Ignorance', who lacked humanity, used to hurt and beat their wives.

"The revered Prophet (S) banned the beating of women, unless in special circumstances when punishment becomes wajib (obligatory)."[200]

"The Prophet (S) also stated: 'I am astonished at a man who beats his wife, whereas it is he himself, more than his wife, who deserves a beating. O people, do not beat your women with sticks because such an act has Qisas (reprisal).'"[201]

Oppressing a woman who has wishfully married her husband, who seeks comfort and tranquility with him, and who expects her husband to share with her problems, is not right. In fact Allah entrusts a woman to her husband through marriage and a man's mistreatment with his wife would be unfaithfulness towards Allah's trust in him.

"Imam Ali (a.s.) stated: 'Women are entrusted to men, and as such are not owners of their fortunes and misfortunes. They are with you like a trust of Allah; so do not hurt them and do not make (the life) difcult for them.'"[202]

A man who hits his wife, inicts such damage on her soul that she might suffer from a complex; and the family love and warmth would almost denitely fade away. How can a man maintain a sound marital relationship with his battered and degraded wife? This is really shameful.

"The Prophet of Allah (S) stated: 'O you (men)! How can any of you

---

[200] Mustadrak, vol 2, p 550.

[201] Bihar al-Anwar, vol 103, p 249

[202] Mustadrak, vol 2, p 551.

beat his wife and there- after embrace her'?"²⁰³

A man, unless having a particular right over his wife, similar to those to be mentioned in this chapter is not lawfully permitted to force his wife into doing anything or to resort to physical punishment upon her disobedience. For instance a woman, lawfully is not duty-bound to carry out housework such as cleaning, cooking, washing up, childcare, knitting, sewing, etc.

Although the majority of women do carry out these works of a housewife on their own, these are not mandatory. Men should be grateful to their wives for their work in the house. Therefore, no man has the right to question or punish his wife when faced with her refusal to carry out the house- keeping chores.

Islam recommends physical punishment of one's wife only in two cases where his rights are violated:

Case 1: A man is Islamically and lawfully allowed to seek sexual satisfaction and pleasure from his wife and to derive all sorts of enjoyment from this relationship. His wife is lawfully duty-bound to yield to her husband's sexual desires. If a woman refuses to satisfy her husband, the husband should initially persuade her in an orderly manner. However, if a man feels that his wife is trying to be malicious to him, and if he cannot tolerate the situation, then by observing the prescribed stages can punish her.

Allah states in the Holy Qur'an:

> *"...And (as to} those on whose part you fear desertion admonish them. and leave them alone in the sleeping places and beat them; then if they obey you do not seek a way against them; surely Allah is High Great." (The Holy Qur'an, 4:34)*

---

[203] Wasa.il al-Shi'ah, vol 14, p 119.

Therefore, the Qur'an allows beating one's wife as the final stage of punishment, in the event of unreasonable behaviour of a woman with regard to the sexual desires of her husband.

The first stage is giving advice. Secondly, the man should avoid sharing her bed or turn his back towards her, and in this way he should show his anger. If nothing positive happens at the end of the second stage and still the woman continues to refuse her husband, he is permitted to beat her (lightly).

A man, however, is not permitted to surpass the prescribed limit and resort to oppression. Men are reminded of the following:

1. The aim of physical punishment of one's wife should be a way of education and not that of taking revenge.
2. Hitting should be done by hand or by using a thin and light wooden stick.
3. Hitting to the extent that results in changing the color of the skin (to blue or red) is not permitted and is punishable by the payment of a Diyah (fine).
4. Hitting of sensitive parts of the body such as the eyes, head, stomach, etc is not permitted.
5. Physical punishment should not be so hard as to create hatred and ill-feeling between the couple, or to drive the wife towards more disobedience.
6. A man (who intends to punish his wife in this manner) should remember that he is to live with his wife and that the family love should not be destroyed.
7. A man is not allowed to hit his wife if there are legitimate reasons for her non-compliance with his wishes. For instance, if she is in the state of menstruation, fasting in the month of *Ramadan*, being in *ihram* (garb for Hajj pilgrimage), or if she is sick. These are acceptable reasons and a man cannot punish his wife for not

complying with his wishes on these occasions.

Case 2: A woman can go out of the house only after obtaining her husband's permission. Going out without permission is lawfully not allowed and committing it is a sin.

A tradition has been reported that the Prophet (S) did not allow any woman to go out of her house without her husband's permission. "He stated: 'Any woman who goes out of her house without her husband's permission, would be subjected to the curse of all the angels in the heavens and all those who see her, be they jinn or human, until the time she returns (to her home).'"[204]

This is the right of any husband which must be observed by their wives.

But men should not be too strict with their wives on this account. It is better for them to allow their wives to go out whenever possible.

This right of men is not meant to be a show of strength or an attempt at putting pressure on their wives, but a means of preventing women from going to undesirable and unsuitable places.

Being too strict, not only is not useful, but may affect the family relationship, or even drive a woman towards disobedience and corruption.

A man must stop his wife from going to corrupt and unsuitable places and gatherings. It is a religious obligation for women to obey their husbands. A disobedient woman can be punished by her husband. Here again the punishment should be carried out in stages.

A woman, however, can go out of the house on specic occasions without her husband's permission and men are not permitted to hurt their wives in such cases:

1. Going out of the house for learning the necessary commandments

---

[204] Ibid, p 154

of religion.
2. Going out of the house for Hajj when she possesses the necessary financial means and ability to perform Hajj.
3. Going out of the house to repay a debt provided it is not possible to repay without going out of the house.

Suspicious Men

It is rightful for men to be watchful of their wives but not to an extent of suspicion and distrust. Some men are suspicious and doubt their wives' faithfulness. This is dangerous and makes life very difcult for all the family.

A man who is suffering, from this behavior, constantly picks up fault with his wife. He monitors her closely and follows her everywhere. He finds supporting evidence for his cause of suspicion from every thing. If he sees his wife talking to a man, or finds a photograph of a man among her belongings, or finds a letter written to her by a man, or finds a man looking at her, he would reach certainty with respect to her unfaithfulness. If his wife hides a letter from him, he would think that it is a love letter. If she expresses her love less than before, he would doubt her sincerity.

He might even think that since his daughter does not look like him, his wife must have committed adultery.

All such examples can be regarded as a firm proof of a woman's infidelity by the suspicious husband. The situation becomes worse if a relative or friend agrees with his suspicion.

Families, who are affected by this illness, suffer a great deal. The man would act like a detective around the house, and his wife would feel as if she was being kept in custody. They would both suffer mentally and their marriage would become endangered. They might even resort to divorce or murder.

There are many cases of homicide and suicide which have occurred as a result of suspicion.

Under these conditions a man and his wife should be aware of the possible grave consequences and, through wisdom and understanding, repel any danger which could threaten their marriage or even their lives. They only need to be a ware of the potential danger and be able to think clearly in order to overcome their problems.

A man should give up his fanaticism and extreme jealousy. He must act logically. He must be aware that convicting his wife of adultery is not a trivial matter, and that such an allegation needs denite proof.

Allah states in the Holy Qur'an:

> *" O you who believe! avoid most of suspicion, for surely suspicion in some cases is a sin..." (The Holy Qur'an, 49:12)*

"The Prophet of Allah (S) stated: 'Whoever, falsely, accuses his wife of committing adultery would lose all the benets from his good deeds just as a snake sheds its skin. And for each hair on his body, one thousand sins would be written down in his record (for the Day of Judgment).'"[205]

"The Prophet of Allah (S) also stated: 'Whoever falsely accuses a faithful man or woman, Allah would, on the Day of Judgment, hold him on a heap of re so that he receives the punishment for his sin.'"[206]

As long as a woman's unfaithfulness is not proved through rm evidence, a man does not have any right to accuse her, otherwise he would be committing a sin for which, as per Islam, he is to be punished with eighty lashes.

Evidence based on purely imaginative grounds are not indicative of any thing. Old letters, pictures, etc do not prove any thing.

---

[205] Bihar al-Anw'ar, vol 103, p 248.

[206] Ibid, vol 75, p 194.

Keeping such things is not right, but this is a mistake that most young people commit and it is not a thing to be seriously concerned with.

If a woman is seen conversing with a stranger, although she is not right in doing so, this isolated event cannot be held against her as a proof of her unfaithfulness. This is because she might have thought it rude not to pay heed to that man, or he might have not been a stranger but a friend of her father or brother.

If a woman makes a compliment to a man, although she should not, it may be out of simplicity and therefore cannot be indicative of her unfaithfulness.

If a woman tells a lie about a relationship, or hides her letters, it may be that there is a good reason for it or she may fear her husband's groundless accusations.

If a woman has grown cold towards her husband, it may be that she is upset with him, that she may be ill, or may have other problems.

In brief, for all situations which may indicate symptoms of unfaithfulness, one can nd tens of good reasons which render the possibility of any wrong doing as void.

Dear Sir! For the sake of Allah stop being suspicious. Consider yourself a fair judge and view the problem with logic. Measure the degree of the possibility of your wife's unfaithfulness and nd out whether it is denite, just a suspicion, or even feasible?

I am not saying that you should be indifferent or careless but that you should act upon the amount of evidence you possess and not more. Why should you exaggerate the problem with baseless suspicion and make life difcult for yourself and your family? How would you feel if anybody accused you in a similar manner? Why do you think in an unfair manner? Why should you disgrace yourself and your wife? Why can you not have mercy upon your wife? Have you ever thought that she might eventually deviate from the right path through your mistrust and false accusations?

"Imam Ali (a.s.) stated to his son, Imam Hasan (a.s.): 'Be careful not to act possessively when you should not. Because this would incline the right people towards corruption and the chaste people towards committing sin.'"[207]

If you are suspicious of your wife, do not discuss it with just anyone whom you see, because they might approve of your suspicion out of enmity, simplicity or carelessness. They might approve of your suspicion out of enmity, simplicity or carelessness. They might even strengthen your suspicion and cause you unhappiness in this world and the life after. You should not, specially inform your mother or sister because they would naturally be in agreement with you and thus increase your suspicion. You must seek advice from wise and experienced friends or relatives.

The best approach, however, is for you to talk to your wife and ask her for an explanation. But you should not seek to prove her guilt. Listen to what she has to tell you and decide like a fair judge who is free from any prejudice.

At least try to believe her and imagine your brother-in-law is presenting you with evidence of your sister's unfaithfulness. Why should you act mercilessly and regard her as a proven criminal'?

Be wise and patient, lest you divorce her on baseless grounds. Suppose you endure the sufferings of a divorce, but how certain are you about the next wife? You would still be suspicious. What is their fault if it is you that is suffering with this illness? Be wise and try to understand your own problem.

Be careful not to resort to commit suicide or murder your wife. Because you would destroy your life here in this world and the Almighty Allah would punish you in the life Hereafter.

You must know that spilling blood would one day be revealed and

---

[207] Ibid, vol 103, p 252.

then you would either be executed or would spend your life in prison.

If you do not agree with this point, then just take a look at the statistics of convicts.

Wives of suspicious men also have a great responsibility with respect to their families. These women must sacrice and prove their ability in such difcult situations.

Dear Madam! First of all your husband is infected with a dangerous illness where he, unwillingly, takes the wrong steps which would endanger your family.

You must express your love for him as much as possible. He must be certain that he is the only man in your life. Be patient with him, do not shout at him, do not refuse to talk to him and do not be stubborn with him.

If you feel that he is monitoring your letters or controlling your comings and goings, do not protest. Tell him every thing, tell the truth. A void lies or denials of the events which have happened. If he ever nds out that you have been lying about anything, he would regard it as a proof of your indelity, the damage of which cannot easily be repaired.

If your suspicious husband ever asks you not to associate with a certain person or wants you to do a certain task, then accept his word, otherwise the cause of his doubt in you would strengthen. In brief, avoid all deeds which could make him suspicious of you.

"Imam Ali (a.s.) stated: 'Whoever exposes himself to accusation, must not blame those who become suspicious of him.'"[208]

If your husband shows animosity towards any one, then you should break your contact with that person altogether.

Dear Madam! It is better for you to keep your family together than keeping your friendship with others. Do not think that you are a slave in the chains of your husband, but realize that you are an ill man's wife.

---

[208] Ibid, vol 74, p 187.

Remember when you made a marital covenant with your husband; you undertook to share all the happy and the sad occasions of life. Is it now fair for you to mistreat your husband who is suffering from an illness? Put away immature thoughts and be provident. By Allah, however much your sacrice for your family, it is worth it. A good woman is one who can cope with in difcult situations.

"Imam as-Sadiq (a.s) stated: 'Jihad of woman is in her patience towards her husband's malicious acts and fervour.'"[209]

Do not do anything which would make your husband suspicious. Do not look at other men.

"The Prophet of Allah (S) stated: ' Allah would be greatly angry with a married woman who lls her eyes with the looks of strangers.'"[210]

Do not associate with strange men. Do not leave the house without your husband's permission. Do not get in strangers' cars. Only your chastity is not enough: but you should seriously avoid anything which would arouse your husband's suspicion. He might become suspicious of the most trivial points of your behaviour.

"A 27-year old woman said in the court: 'It was the winter of 1963, when on a snowy day, I got in a car which belonged to my friend's uncle. She offered that her uncle would give me a lift home. I accepted and got in his car. When we reached home, my husband was standing by the door of the house and since I did not want him to see me in another man's car, I asked my friend's uncle to drive on, which he did. Later, my husband who had seen me in that car, asked about it, but I denied everything. He became more suspicious and it reached a stage where he did not even believe my friend's witness. Now it is eight years that he has neither lived with me nor divorced me. I do not know what

---

[209] Wasa'il al-Shiah, vol 14, p III

[210] Bihar al-Anwar, vol 104, p 39

to do.'"²¹¹

Who do you think is to blame in this story?

I would say that the woman is more guilty than her husband. It is she who, out of carelessness and simplicity, had placed herself and her husband in this situation.

First of all she should not have accepted a lift from a stranger as this is not a correct thing to do for any woman. It is not proper and it may be dangerous.

Secondly, she should not have acted the way she did when she saw her husband. She should have stopped the car and should have explained to her husband.

Thirdly, one of her mistakes was to tell the driver to drive on.

Fourthly, she should not have denied it later. She could have explained every thing even at this late stage and it could have helped to solve the problem.

Of course the man is not right either. He must not regard this event as a conclusive evidence of his wife's guilt. He must consider the possibility that his wife might have carelessly got in a stranger's car and then she might have, fearfully, asked the driver not to stop and naturally denied the whole affair.

He must investigate the matter and once he is certain that she is not guilty, he must be forgiving.

The Unfaithful Woman

Once a woman, through rm proof, is convicted of adultery, her husband would be placed in a very difcult situation. On the one hand, his honor is endangered and on the other, enduring such a disgrace is not easy. He feels trapped in a state of deadlock from which an easy escape is

---

[211] Ittela'at, 23rd Esfand, 1350 Solar Hijri.

not possible. A man in this situation can choose one of the following:

a) He can keep silent about the affair in order to save his honor and for the sake of his family. But he must live with this event for the rest of his life. Of course this choice cannot be acceptable by any honorable man, since it would not be possible for him to cope with his adulterous wife and a possible illegitimate child.

Passion is an admirable quality of men, so much so that a man without it would not enjoy the grace of the Almighty Allah as well as being dishonored by the people who know him.

What a disgraceful and shameful life those men have who are indifferent with regard to their wives' disloyalties.

"The Prophet of Allah (S) stated: 'The fragrance of Paradise can be smelt at a distance of ve hundred years journey, but two groups of people are deprived from it; those which are disowned by their parents and the cuckold ones'. It was asked: 'O Prophet (S) of Allah: 'Who is a cuckold'? The Prophet (S) replied: 'A man who knows his wife is an adulterer (and remains silent about it).'"[212]

b) He could kill either or both his wife and the man she committed adultery with. He can take his revenge and nd peace. But this is a dangerous act and would not have a good end, because a murder would rarely be concealed for ever. A murderer would nally be found and be punished. He cannot easily prove his wife's disloyalty in the court either; and thus the possibility of his release from imprisonment would be very remote. He might even receive capital punishment. Thus he would lose his life and his children would go astray. Therefore, it is not wise for a man to endanger his life just for the sake of seeking revenge.

He should be wise and prudent and be able to control his temper until he can nd a suitable solution to his problem.

c) He can commit suicide in order to get rid of himself from his

---

[212] Wasa'il al-Shiah, vol 14, p 109

wife's disloyalty and leave a disgraceful life. This is not a wise act either, because on the one hand he has murdered himself, which itself is a major sin in Islam and the murderer would be punished by Allah on the Day of Judgment. On the other hand, he would have deprived himself from life. What kind of logic is it that would suggest self-killing as a revenge for someone else's guilt. He would suffer in the next life as well as give more freedom to his wife to commit more adulterous acts.

d) He could divorce her. This is the wisest thing to do. It is right that a divorce would destroy his family life and would inict much harm upon him and his children, but there is not any other way. It is better for him to divorce her and take the children, because it is not right to leave them with a corrupt woman to bring up.

Of course bringing up children is not an easy job for a man, but he must be sure that Allah would help him. He could help him lead an honorable life.

Do not Go After Other Women

A man must do his utmost to choose a woman that is suitable for him. He is in a position where he can exercise care and caution in nding a partner whom he is going to live with for the rest of his life. He, however, after marriage, should not go after other women. He must not think of any woman except his wife.

He must realize that a girl has left her family to live with him and it is not right for him to pursue childish desires. He must make efforts in bringing his new family together and must try to create a friendly atmosphere at home.

A man who is interested in his own happiness, must, after marriage, give up naive thoughts and must adapt himself to a new life.

It is senseless for a married man to joke with other women or express his affection for them. A man would also not like his wife to joke with men, A woman would not like this type of attitude of her husband towards other women.

A woman who sees her husband close to other women would feel jealous and would be disheartened. She would lose interest in her house and family. She might retaliate with a similar action or seek divorce.

"A woman complained about her husband to the court. She had been married for thirty-three years and said that her husband had always been in the habit of jesting with other women."[213]

"A woman complained to the court that her husband was always expressing interest in her friends. She said that she could not invite her friends to the house because they thought her husband was having an interest in them and that she was embarrassed because of him."[214]

It is not proper for a married man to have an eye on other women. Ogling and having eyes at other women results in internal anxiety, nervousness and indifference towards one's family.

Allah states in the Holy Qur'an:

"Say to the believing men that they cast down their looks and guard their private parts..." (The Holy Qur'an, 24:30)

Imam as-Sadiq (a.s) stated: 'A lewd look is a poisonous arrow thrown by Satan. It is likely that such a glance would be the cause of sorrow and grief for some time.'"[215]

Flirting is regarded as an illness by psychiatrists. An eye which has become used to this habit, would never be satised. Looking in this manner becomes a cause of many corruptions, where the youth can

---

[213] Ittela'at, 26th Bahman, 1350 Solar Hijri
[214] Ibid, 27th Bahman, 1348 Solar Hijri
[215] Wasa'il al-Shiah, vol 14, p 138

deviate from the right path. What the eyes do not see the heart would not desire.

One might initially resist the grave consequences of forbidden glances, but nally he may break down, and become inuenced by what he has seen.

"Imam as-Sadiq (a.s.) stated: 'Frequent (forbidden) looks create lust in one's heart, and this is sufcient for deviating the looker.'"[216]

Islam, knowing the harm of such lewd looks, has forbidden it altogether.

A man who suddenly sees a woman in the streets or elsewhere, should at once direct his look somewhere else or close his eyes. He should not persist in staring at women. This may be difcult at rst, but with a little practice he can do it.

Wise people know that preventing oneself from forbidden looks would remove many potential dangers such as murder, crime, suicide, divorce, nervous breakdown, mental disorders, weakness or heart, anxiety, family rows, etc.

I am aware of the difculties that the youth are confronted with at this age, and I know that closing one's eyes to obscene scenes in the streets and elsewhere is not easy, but there is not any way other than to ignore them.

A man who can close his eyes to other women, would be protected from many corruptions. Instead he would enjoy his family and peace of mind.

Dear Sir! If you are after happiness, once married, do not take notice of other women. Do not make compliments to other women in front of your wife. Do not say: "I wish I had married Miss…; missed many good opportunities…"

Such statements would hurt your wife and she would grow cold

---

[216] Ibid, p 139

towards you and life. She might even try to do the same and talk similarly.

As a result your life would lack happiness. Pitiful are those men, who for a few moments of lust, chase after corrupt women and leave their own chaste wives, as if they have never known family love and sincerity. Such men are like animals who have only concentrated on eating, sleeping, and lust. They seem to be strangers to humanity and affection.

Be Grateful

Housework may possibly seem an easy job to some men, but it is only fair to acknowledge it as a hard and tedious job.

A housewife, even if she works all day and night, would not be able to nish all her work. Cooking, cleaning, washing the clothes and ironing, washing the dishes and arranging them, making the beds, and arranging the furniture and above all taking care of children, not one day, but everyday is very difcult.

A man might think that his wife is just cooking food three times a day and forgets about the rest of her work.

Only a man who is prepared to stay in the house for a month and do the housework would know the pressures involved. He would then appreciate his wife's efforts.

A housewife does all this work happily but she expects her husband to appreciate her and to show his gratitude.

Dear Sir! What is wrong with thanking your wife for her housekeeping? Why should you not express your fondness for the food she cooks? What is wrong with thanking her with regard to her efforts in taking care of your children? Are you not aware that your appreciation for her would encourage and refresh her?

If you remain indifferent to her efforts, or do not show your gratitude, she would lose interest in the housework and then you would complain about her. You should know that you could be the cause of your wife's indolence.

If a stranger does you a small favour, you would thank him many times, but upon your wife's many favours you are not even thanking her once! You are not prepared to even make her happy by showing your appreciation for all her efforts.

"A twenty-nine year old housewife wrote from Tehran: 'I am married to an ungrateful and an inappreciative man who ignores my housework altogether. I wash, clean, cook, decorate the house, knit jumpers for the family, polish his shoes, iron his clothes, etc and he has not even once thanked me.

Whenever I talk to him about the work in the house, he interrupts me and says that I should not praise it before him. He belittles my efforts, whereas his success is mostly due to my hard work.'"[217]

Some men regard it as a manly act to ignore their wives' housework. They think if they make compliments to their wives for their work, the women would be spoiled. They might even believe that a man and wife do not need to thank each other.

This belief is not right, because any good-doer from a psychological point of view, needs appreciation and gratitude. Appreciation encourages one to do good, and this is especially true for a housewife who is doing a tedious job everyday over and over again.

Thus Islam regards being thankful as a good quality in one's behaviour.

"Imam as-Sadiq (a.s) stated: 'Whoever praises a Muslim, Allah would write many praises for him until the Day of Judgment.'"[218]

"The Prophet (S) of Islam stated: 'Whoever respects a Muslim, and

---

[217] "Wa Nami Danand Chara.. ("And They Do Not Know, Why?"). p 140.
[218] Shafi, vol 1 p 197.

speaks affably to him, and removes his sorrow, would always be under the blessings of Allah.'"[219]

Be Clean at Home Also

Observing cleanliness is necessary for everyone everywhere. One must always keep his body and clothes clean. He must bathe himself at least once a week and must wash his face and hands with soap and water every morning. He must brush his teeth, comb his hair, trim his hair, wash his feet wear clean socks everyday and must also wear pure clothes. The holy religion of Islam emphasizes greatly about cleanliness and being well-dressed.

The Prophet of Allah (S) stated: 'Cleanliness is a part of the faith (of Islam).'"[220]

"The Holy Prophet (S) saw a man who was dirty, had messy hair and looked unattractive. The Prophet (S) stated: 'Using the blessings of Allah is a part of the faith (of Islam).'"[221]

"The Prophet (S) of Islam also stated: 'A dirty person would be a bad worshipper of Allah.'"[222]

"In addition, the Holy Prophet (S) stated: *'Jibra'il* (Gabriel) laid so much stress on brushing the teeth that I feared for them.'"[223]

"Imam Ali (a.s.) stated: 'Allah is beautiful and he likes beauty. And he also likes to see the effect of his blessings on his servants.'"[224]

Cleanliness and beauty is not only for women, but men should, also

---

[219] Ibid

[220] Bihar al-Anwar, vol 62, p 129

[221] Shafi, vol l, p 208

[222] Ibid

[223] Ibid, p 210.

[224] Ibid, p 212

be clean and well-dressed. Some men are not bothered about their cleanliness and take a bath only once in a while. They do not care for the state of their clothes and do not bother about trimming their beards. They smell badly and thus make others keep away from them.

Those men who are careful about cleanliness and do lay importance on their clothing, mostly do so outside their own houses. That is they look clean and well-dressed outside the house for the people, not inside their homes for their families. They appear very smart in the streets, gatherings, etc but as soon as they return home, they change into worn out clothes. They rarely attend to the state of their hair and faces at home for the sake of their families.

They might not even bother to wash their faces before eating breakfast. Men of this kind make their families not bother to look at them.

Dear Sir! if you cannot tolerate a dirty and shabby dressed wife, and you expect her to look clean and beautiful at home, then be sure that she expects the same from you. She, too, hates the sight of a dirty, smelly and untidy husband. She also likes to see you clean and smart.

If you do not satisfy her expectations with regard to smartness, then she would notice other men who are clean and smart and she might even think they are from another world. She compares you with them and might lose interest in you. Therefore, try to look good at home as well as outside.

Your wife would not notice other men if you were successful in drawing her attention toward yourself. Why should you look good for strangers in the streets but look messy before your wife and children?

Therefore, the holy religion of Islam orders men to adorn themselves for their wives.

"The Prophet (S) of Islam stated: 'It is obligatory for a man to provide his wife with food and clothing, and not to appear before her with an unpleasant appearance. If he did (the above mentioned), then he would take care of her rights.'"²²⁵

"The Prophet of Allah (S) also stated: 'You (men) must make yourselves tidy and be prepared for your wives, as you would like them (your women) to be prepared for you.'"²²⁶

"Hasan ibn Jiham says: 'I saw Hadrat Abu al-Hasan (a.s.) who had dyed his hair. I asked if indeed he had dyed his hair'. He stated: 'Yes, adornment of man (for the sake of his wife) helps her keep her chastity. Women who deviate from the path of chastity do so due to the carelessness and faults of their husbands.' Hadrat Abu al-Hasan then stated: 'Do you like to see your wife untidy?' I replied: '.No.' He then added: 'She thinks just as you do.'"²²⁷

"Imam Rida (a.s.) stated: 'Women of the Bani Israel deviated from the path of chastity because their men were not bothered about cleanliness and their good looks.' The Imam then added: 'What you expect of your wife, she expects the same from you.'"²²⁸

Nurse Your Wife

The husband and wife always need each other's cooperation and expression of love. However, this need becomes more intense at times of illness and on other similar occasions. An ill person, just as he needs a doctor and medicine, requires nursing and loving care. A good nurse would be able to help a patient recover better and faster.

A woman also expects her husband to nurse her when she is bed-ridden. She expects him to care for her more than her parents.

A woman who works at home like a maid, deserves such loving care

---

[225] Bihar al-Anwar, vol 103, p 254

[226] Mustadrak, vol 2, p 559

[227] Wasa'il al-Shiah, vol 14, p 183

[228] Bihar al-Anwar, vol 76, p 102.

from her husband. She rightly expects her husband to take care of her.

Paying for treatment and medicine is one of the usual expenditures of life and a man is duty-bound to provide her with the necessary money. A woman who is working at home without any wages, certainly has a right to expect her husband to pay for her treatment.

There are men who are shamelessly unfair. They use their wives when they are healthy and able, but refuse to pay money when they are ill. Any little money men spend for their wives' treatment is accompanied by many complaints. Some men, if they feel the cost of treatment is high, might even lose their wives. Is this behaviour really fair?

"A woman was complaining about her husband. She said: 'I was working hard at home and went through many happy and harsh times with my husband. However, now that I have become ill my husband wants to leave me.'"[229]

Dear Sir! if you are interested in your happiness and your family's prosperity, you must take your wife to a doctor when she becomes ill. You must pay for her treatment. Moreover, you must nurse her kindly. Now that she has left her parents to live with you, she expects you to be more loving to her than her parents. She is your partner and the mother of your children. Sympathize with her and make her hopeful of a speedy recovery. Cook for her. Prepare suitable food and buy the prescribed items. Feed her. All this will make her happy.

Keep the children quiet. Be watchful of her at night. Whenever she is awake ask how she is. If she cannot sleep because of pain, then stay up with her. You can even ask your children to help you look after their mother. Do not ever leave your wife unattended, especially when she is in pain.

At such times, your wife would notice your love and would in turn

---

[229] Ittela'at, 18th Urdibahisht, 1351 Solar Hijri.

love you more. She would be proud of you and would attend to you and the children more, once she is healthy again.

"The Prophet (S) of Islam stated: 'The best of you is the one who is better towards his family, and I am to my family the best among all.'"[230]

"The Prophet (S) of Islam also stated: 'Whoever makes efforts to realize a wish of an ill person, would be puried from his sins, just as the day he was born'. One of the Ansars (helpers who helped the Prophet settle in Madinah) asked: 'O Prophet (S) of Allah! May my parents be sacriced for you, what if the ill person is from amongst your family (Ahl al-Bayt)? Is there not more reward in this case?' The Prophet of Allah (S) replied: 'Yes.'"[231]

Family Economy

To arrange for alimony of wife is wajib (obligatory) for husband. That is a man is duty-bound to pay for the expenses of his wife such as food, clothes, house, doctor, and medicine. He would be wrong not to maintain his wife and could be prosecuted by law.

One cannot expect a family to live without any expense. They all need food, medicine, clothes, and a place to live in. However, they might ask for unnecessary items in which case one can disobey them and not conform with their various desires.

A wise man would spend according to his earnings. He must classify the necessary commodities and purchase them in the order of priority whenever he can. He must also save some money for a rainy day. Some money must be put away for the house rent or purchasing a new place. He must not forget the electricity, water, gas, and telephone bills. Taxes have to be paid and school fees must be kept in mind. He must seriously

---

[230] Wasa'il al-Shiah, vol 14. p 122

[231] Ibid, vol 2, p 643

avoid overspending and not pay for unimportant items. A calculated manner of spending would never confront one with bankruptcy or debt.

Allah regards balanced spending as a sign of faith and states in the Holy Qur'an:

"And they who when they spend are neither extravagant nor parsimonious and (keep) between these the just mean." (The Holy Qur'an, 25:67)

"Imam as-Sadiq (a.s) stated: 'I guarantee a person. Who spends moderately, would never become poor.'"[232]

"Imam as-Sadiq (a.s) also stated: 'There are four groups of people whose prayers would not reach the level of acceptance; one group of persons is that which wastes his wealth and then asks the Almighty Allah, O Allah! give me my sustenance. Then Allah replies, had I not ordered you to observe moderation (in your expenditure).'"[233]

"Abdullah ibn Aban says: 'I asked Musa ibn J'afar (a.s) about maintaining one's family and he stated: 'Extravagance and niggardliness are both abominable. One must not lose moderation.'"[234]

A wise man would avoid borrowing money and would not take a loan for unessential purposes. An economy which is based on loans (with interests), received from banks and other establishments is Islamically and logically wrong and is not praiseworthy.

Buying goods on hire-purchase system, although makes your house look good, but takes away your comfort and peace of mind.

Why should one buy unnecessary goods more expensively and ll the

---

[232] Wasa'il al-Shiah, vol 15, p 258.

[233] Ibid, p 261.

[234] Ibid

pockets of bankers by installments? What kind of a life is it when every thing is acquired at a hire- purchase price? Is it not better for one to wait and save his money in order to buy goods at cheaper prices?

It is true that earning money is difcult and it affects one's life a great deal, however, more important is the way in which one spends his money. There are families with good earnings who are always under debts of others. There are also many families with low earnings who live comfortably. The difference between the two is the way they spend their earnings. Therefore, it is advantageous to a family that the man either takes control of expenditures or supervises the one who is responsible for it.

Finally, it is reminded that meanness is just as bad as overspending. If a man has more earnings he must make his family more comfortable and provide their essential requirements as much as possible.

Wealth and money are all for spending and providing the necessities of life, and not for piling up and leaving them behind in this world.

The signs of wealth must be apparent in one's family and house. What is the use of working hard and not spending?

One must use his wealth with regard to his family and his own comfort. It is hateful to see someone who is able money wise but his children long for good food and clothes. Children of a stingy person would wait for his death to share his wealth.

If the Almighty Allah bestows his blessings onto someone, this blessing must be apparent in that person's life.

"The Prophet (S) of Islam stated: 'He is not one of us (followers of Prophet (S) who possesses money but keeps his family away from his wealth.'"[235]

"Musa ibn J'afar (a.s) stated: 'A man's family members are his dependents. Thus whoever is bestowed with the blessings of Allah,

---

[235] Mustadrak, vol 2, p 643

should expand on his dependents' comfort, or else such blessings may be taken away from him.'"[236]

Imam Rida (a.s) stated: 'It is worthy of a man to grant his family-members with comfort by his spending, so that they do not await his death.'"[237]

"Imam Ali (a.s.) stated: 'Arrange fruits for your dependents every Friday so that they may be pleased with the coming of Friday.'"[238]

Extend Your Help in the Household Works

Although housekeeping is a duty of women, it must be realized that running the affairs of a house is not an easy task

A housewife, however much time she spends on housekeeping, would not be able to do it all This is especially true when one has to entertain one's guests or when one becomes ill, etc Housekeeping is tiresome for a housewife and thus husbands are expected to assist their wives in this respect.

It is not fair that a man sits around the house idly while his wife remains busy in so much works It is only proper for him to help his wife as much as possible whenever he can. This help is a sign of affection which attracts one's wife to her husband and family.

It is not at all a manly act that a man should not touch anything around the house, or orders his wife around A house is not a command headquarters, but a place of love, kindness, and cooperation.

Dear Sir! Do not think that working at home is degrading On the contrary, through your assistance, your wife would appreciate you more

---

[236] Bihar al-Anwar, vol l04, p 69

[237] Wasa'il al-Shi'ah, vol 15, p 249

[238] Bihar al-Anwar, vol 14, p 73.

The Prophet (S) of Islam. Who is the most revered person in history, used to help in the housework.'"[239]

Ayeshah, the wife of the Prophet (S) said :'Whenever the Prophet (S) was free from his work, he used to sew his clothes, repair his shoes and used to work at home like other men.'[240]

Return Home Soon

An unmarried man is free to spend his time. But once married, he must alter his program. He cannot stay out for any length of time that he desires He should inform his wife of his whereabouts, etc. He must not forget that his wife stays at home all the day, cleans the house, washes the dishes, and cooks. She waits for him to return home as soon as his work is nished, to see him, talk to him, and to enjoy his company. The children look forward to seeing their father too. It is not fair that a man should leave his family at home and pursue his enjoyment somewhere else.

Marriage is not only providing food and clothes for one's family. A woman is her husband's partner and not a servant. She is not there to work all the day and get fed in return, but rather she hopes to have a permanent friend and partner.

Some men are truly unfair, unjust, and foolish. They leave their wives and children at home and spend their nights somewhere else. The money that they should spend at home for the family, they waste at other places. Such men have not yet understood the meaning of love and affection and regard their cheap and lthy enjoyments as a way of good living. They overlook the fact that they would degrade themselves through such deeds. Others would recognize them as silly

---

[239] Bihar al-Anwar, vol 16, p 227.

[240] Ibid, p 230.

and impudent.

These men are the causes of the unhappiness of themselves and their families. Their acts drive their wives to seek a divorce from them.

"A man who had divorced his wife, said in the court: 'At the beginning of my marriage, I had certain friends that I used to go out with, while leaving my wife behind…, and I used to return home in the early hours of the morning, My wife, who was fed up with this situation, obtained a divorce. We had ten children, whom I was supposed to meet twice a month. Some time passed like this. But it is quite some time now that my children are in hiding and I am desperate to see my children.'"[241]

"A woman said: 'I am frustrated with loneliness. My husband does not care about me at all. Every night for his own enjoyment he is out until the early hours of the morning.'"[242]

Dear sir! you are now married. You should not act like a bachelor. You are responsible for your wife and the children. Do not associate with unworthy friends. Return home as soon as you finish your work.

Enjoy a family life and be a good company for your wife and the children. Even if your nightly amusements are not wrong they can be nevertheless harmful to you and your married life.

Be Faithful

Upon a marital covenant, the individual lives of two persons converge into a single social joint life. The holy covenant of marriage means that a man and a woman promise each other to be together for the rest of their lives, to help each other, to be kind and understanding at all times, for richer and poorer, in sickness and in health, happiness and sorrow, etc.

---

[241] Ittela'at, 11th Tir, 1349 Solar Hijri

[242] "Wa Nami Danand Chara" (..And They Do Not Know, Why?") p, 138

Humanity demands that one should remain faithful to one's promises. A married couple should not forget their treaty at difcult times.

A young girl, who chooses one man to live with her for the rest of her life, expects him not to leave her at an age when she is no longer a young woman any more. It is not fair that a man should seek pleasure with anyone other than his wife.

A woman who contributes a great deal in building a strong family with good economical prospects, does not expect her husband to go after another woman.

A woman who works hard at home, naturally hopes that her husband would not deprive her of his love and affection at times of sickness and inability to work. The least she expects of him is not to go after his pleasure alone.

Some men are truly emotionless. When their wives are young and good-looking they enjoy their company, but leave them when they lose their good look.

A man divorced his wife on the basis of her being bad-omen, because since their marriage his father had died and his uncle had become bankrupt.'"[243]

"A man who had married a young woman out of love, divorced her later on the grounds that he did not love her.'"[244]

"A woman Mrs… complained to the court: 'For years I have lived with my husband, but now that I have become ill, he says that he does not want a sick wife.'"[245]

Dear Sir! You are not an animal whose life is all about eating and lust. You are a human being with emotion, conscience and sacricial characteristics. Is it really fair that you pursue your enjoyment away

---

[243] Ittela'at, 25th Dey, 1350 Solar Hijri

[244] Ibid, 26th Shahrivar, 1348 Solar Hijri

[245] Ibid, 18th Urdibahisht, 1351 Solar Hijri

from your wife? If yes, then you are an oppressor and as such you would be punished in this very world. If you spend your time with another woman, then for the sake of a few minutes of enjoyment, you may indeed lose your peace of mind and would be affected by nervousness. Besides you would be disgraced before people. Your children would not accept you either and would react by being malicious to you.

If your wife ever becomes ill, take the necessary steps to cure her, and if she has an incurable illness, then stay with her, sacrice yourself and do not remarry while she is still alive.

Do not disappoint her during the difcult times. What would you expect if you were in her situation? It is only fair that she would expect the same from you.

Is it right that your wife, when you are ill, should seek a divorce? Would she not be disgraced in the eyes of your friends and relatives? So if you agree that faithfulness and sincerity are good, then try to be faithful.

Education and Training

A young newly married woman has the responsibility of running the affairs of her husband and as such she would need knowledge of cooking, cleaning, ironing, sewing, arranging the furniture, entertaining her guests, socializing with others, taking care of her child, etc.

Her husband would expect her to know all of this. However, his expectations may not be realized most of the time because his young wife's knowledge about housekeeping is either non-existent or very little indeed.

What can one do? This is a problem in our societies. Neither the parents are bothered, nor the educational system contains enough programs to meet this need. Nevertheless one should nd a solution to this problem.

A man, since intending to live with his wife for the rest of his life, must help educate her, because usually men are older than their wives and thus more experienced.

A man, through patience, can educate his wife and teach her things that he knows. He can even ask his mother, sister or aunts about things that he does not know or can even buy books on the related subjects like cooking, tailoring, housekeeping, etc.

A man must also encourage his wife to read the books which may prove to be morally helpful. He must correct her moral shortcomings with good manners and not by protesting, or else she would react against him.

A man, through patience, can educate his wife according to his own way of living within the rst two years of their marriage. He may not be successful one hundred percent but undoubtedly would be near satisfaction.

Such education needs patience, time, and wisdom, but a man should try to achieve it. This is because a good partner and a good mother for his children is a blessing for a man.

One of the important points that a Muslim married man should remember is the fact that his wife is also a Muslim and may be unaware of the Islamic code of life and laws. She may not even know about having wuzu (ablution), praying, etc.

As a matter of fact it is a duty of parents to teach their children all the necessary Islamic matters and precepts, unfortunately; however, parents are mostly ignorant of this fact and without teaching their daughters any thing about Islam, marry them off. Thus their responsibility falls upon the shoulders of the men they marry.

Dear Sir! It is your responsibility to familiarize your wife with Islamic precepts and to teach her the dos and don'ts of the religion. Make her learn about Islamic behaviour. If you cannot do this then seek help from others or arrange for books and articles on Islam and make her read and practice them. You can even arrange her education and training through an honest and learned person.

In brief, it is a responsibility of a man to encourage his wife to do good and to forbid her from committing any wrong. If he conforms with this responsibility then he would enjoy the company of a well-behaved, kind, moral, and wise wife.

If he, however, neglects his duty, he would suffer by having an ignorant wife whose faith is weak and who is not immune from immorality. He would also be questioned by Allah in the next world regarding his negligence.

Allah states in the Holy Qur'an:

> *"O you who believe! Save yourselves and your families from a re whose fuel is men and stones…" (The Holy Qur'an, 66:6)*

"Imam as-Sadiq (a.s) stated: 'When the above Ayah (verse) was revealed, one of the Muslims was crying and said: 'I am unable to save even myself from the Hellre and I am supposed to be responsible to save my family from Hell as well'! The Prophet (S) stated to this man: 'It would sufce you only to order them to do those things that you have to do yourself and to forbid them from those deeds that you yourself should abstain from.'"[246]

"The Holy Prophet (S) stated: 'Men have been made guardians and responsible for their families and as such they are responsible for their dependents.'"[247]

"The Holy Prophet (S) has also reminded women: 'Invite your husbands to do good before they persuade you to commit wrong

---

[246] Wasa'il al-Shi'ah, vol 11, p 417

[247] Mustadrak, vol 2, p 550.

deeds.'"[248]

Having A Child

One of the possible sore points for a couple is having a child. That is a woman may want to have a child but her husband disagrees or vice versa. This problem sometimes becomes very serious as a result of which a couple may resort to divorce.

"Mrs… made a complaint to the court and said: 'I married at the age of twenty-seven years when my husband had just graduated from the university. He was a lecturer in one of the universities and I felt that I was a lucky woman. However, my husband disagrees with having a child. I do not understand him because we are both healthy and have enough money to at least bring up two children.

He does not dislike children and treats his nieces and nephews well. I am thirty years old and naturally I wish I were a mother. He understands my feelings but says that a child would be a cause of inconvenience in our lives, and so on'. This woman, while stopping herself from crying, is confronted with a problem which is so serious that the couple has decided for a divorce, so that she would remarry while he would have enough time for his scientic research."[249]

Love for children and reproduction is a natural desire of human beings and even of animals. Children are the fruit of life and the best legacy of mankind.

The life of one who has children would not be ended by his death but rather would be continued as if with an extended life. A person without a child or children would feel lonely and forlorn and would feel even worse in old age.

---

[248] Bihar al-Anwar, vol 103, p 227

[249] Ittela'at, 28th Bahman, 1350 Solar Hijri.

A house without children is a place of boredom, and would lack warmth and love. A marriage would always be in danger of breaking down if there were no children. Thus children are the source of family warmth and survival.

"Imam as-Sadiq (a.s.) stated: 'One's happiness is in having children.'"[250]

"The Prophet (S) of Islam stated: 'Give birth to many children because on the Day of Judgment I will take pride in your numbers over the other Ummahs (nations).'"[251]

Love for a child is a natural desire, but some people are deviated from their natural 'self' and are affected by an illness where they bring up different excuses, such as the lack of money, for not having children. However, Allah guarantees that He would give sustenance to all His creatures.

"Bakr ibn Saleh said: 'I wrote a letter to Hadrat Abu al- Hasan (a.s.) saying that I had been taking preventive measures against having a child for ve years, because my wife had been reluctant to have one, and that she was saying, lack of money would make it difcult for us to bring up a child.' I asked Hadrat Abu al-Hasan his opinion on this matter. He replied: 'Do not prevent having a child, because the Almighty Allah would provide him sustenance.'"[252]

Allah would even increase a family's sustenance due to the blessings of children. There are many people who were in difculty before having their children, but found a comfortable life afterwards.

Some people regard children as inconvenient. This is not true and as a matter of fact children are the best source of enjoyment and amusement for the parents.

---

[250] Wasa'il al-Shi'ah, vol 15, p 97.

[251] Ibid, p 96.

[252] Ibid, p 99.

Of course taking care of children is not without difculty and trouble, but since it conforms with the law of nature, one can cope with all the difculties and as such it is worth taking the trouble involved.

How narrow-minded are those men and women who for the sake of not having children resort to divorce!

Is it not really surprising that a man, and that too an educated one for that matter, should disagree with the laws of nature so persistently that he would even be prepared to divorce his wife?

Some couples do not disagree on having a child but argue over the time of having one. A woman or a man of this kind would say: "One must be free at a young age as a child would deprive one from being at liberty to enjoy oneself. It is better to wait until later to have one or two children". If both husband and wife are not of the same opinion, then arguments would start which may end in a divorce.

Let us remember that if one wants children, then this should be achieved at the earliest possible age. This is because children born from young parents are in some respects better off than those born from older parents. Firstly, these children are healthier and stronger. Secondly, since they are from younger parents, they can live for more time with their parents.

They can be better educated and brought up. But children from older parents might become deprived of their parents' guidance and teachings due to their death or disability. Thirdly, children of younger parents would reach an age of forming their own family and taking up jobs, while their parents are still alive.

Thus they can be a great deal of help to their parents when they are old.

In brief, having children at a young age is better than at an older age. But this is not so important that it should cause rows or divorce. It is better for the husband or wife to agree mutually and not let it create a rift in their marriage. Some couples disagree on the number of children they would like.

"A woman, while holding a baby in her arms, said:, After four years of marriage I had two daughters with my husband, but since he wanted a son I became pregnant once more and again gave birth to a girl. I now have three daughters. My husband works in a bank and his salary does not sufce our family. He has recently been insisting that I should become pregnant many times until I give birth to a son.

But I am not prepared for this because his earnings are not enough for us to educate our children the way we want. I have told him many times that boys and girls are both good. I fear that if I become pregnant again I shall give birth to another girl. I am sure that he would again insist on having another child. We cannot agree on this matter and thus have taken our case to the court.'"[253]

It is right that providing for education and training of many children is difcult and this is especially true in the case of those whose earnings are not high.

Therefore, it is better that couples decide on the number of children according to their moral and nancial abilities. They must have understanding and be able to solve their problems through wisdom and kindness. It is not correct for either of them to insist on something illogical.

This problem is not so serious and should not lead a couple to have quarrels or resort to a divorce. There are many families who either have many children or are satised with only one or two.

Some couples have differences about the sex of their proposed children. Some couples, men and women prefer having a son and do not take too kindly to having girls. The birth of a daughter would make a woman feel guilty and therefore she would keep silence because she was the one who has given birth. But the man might express his

---

[253] Ittela'at, 2nd Murdad, 1351 Solar Hijri.

dissatisfaction.

Men are different. Some do not express their dissatisfaction openly and just show a grim face. They do not particularly attend to their wives during the post-natal days. They look sad. Some men, however, react severely to the news of having a daughter. They become angry with their wives and pick up fault with them. They protest and create a row. Some men go further and might even beat them up or even divorce them.

"A woman said in the court: 'I got married fteen months ago and became pregnant six months later. Recently, when the time for delivery was near, my husband said to me that I had to give birth to a son. But I felt that I might have twins or even triplets. A few days ago I gave birth to twin girls. I was very happy about it. When my husband came to know about the birth, he was upset and left the room. Later, when I asked him to take the girls home he shouted at me and blamed me for delivering twin girls. He asked me to leave him. so I went to my parents and now I am applying for divorce." [254]

"Mrs… said to a reporter in the court: 'After twenty-one years of marriage and having ve children. I have to leave a life to which I have contributed so much to for another woman a woman who is able to give birth to a boy. I have ve beautiful and talented daughters who are no problem to their father at all. What is my guilt if I cannot give birth to a boy? My husband is blaming me for it and wants me to allow him to remarry with another woman'.[255]

Unfortunately, this quality has remained with some people from the time of *Jahiliyyah* (age of ignorance) that they doubt the human nature of the female sex. They arc ashamed of having daughters and feel belittled. In the age of ignorance, people used to bury their baby

---

[254] Ibid, 14th Tir, 1349 Solar Hijri.

[255] Ibid, 16th Esfand, 1350 Solar Hijri.

daughters alive. The Holy Qur'an mentions their deeds and states:

> "And when a daughter is announced to one of them, his face becomes black and he is full of wrath." (The Holy Qur'an, 16:58)

> "He hides himself from the people because of the evil of that which is announced to him. Shall he keep it with disgrace or bury it (alive) in the dust? Now surely evil is what they judge." (The Holy Qur'an, 16:59)

But Islam denounces this wrong idea and regards men and women as equal.

"The Prophet (S) of Islam stated: 'The best of your children are your daughters.'"[256]

"The Prophet (S) of Islam also stated: 'The sign of a lucky woman is that her rst child is a girl.'"[257]

"In addition, the Holy Prophet (S) stated: 'Whoever looks after three daughters or three sisters, Paradise would become incumbent upon him.'"[258]

If a girl was inferior, Allah would not have made his (Prophet's (SA)) descendants line continue through Hadrat Zahra (a.s).

Dear Sir: you are claiming to be a civilized and modern human being, so abstain from having such evil thoughts. What difference does it make if you have a girl or a boy? They are both your offspring and both can advance towards perfection. A girl also can become a prominent personality through your correct care and education.

---

[256] Mustadrak, vol 2, p 615

[257] Ibid, p 614.

[258] Wasa'il al-Shi'ah, vol 15, p 100

A girl is in some respects better than a boy.

Firstly, a girl is more sympathetic to their parents. Boys usually do not benet their parents when they grow up and become independent. Girls, if parents do not place any preference on their sons, would be more loving towards them.

Secondly, a girl requires less expense as compared to a boy, because she generally spends less time in her parents' house since she gets married at an earlier age and leaves her parents with only a few items for her new life. But boys become young men who may stay with their parents for a long time. The parents would have to pay for his education, nd him a job, may have to pay his expenses during his two years of military service, wherever necessary, and then marry him off to a young woman, after which he would need to be provided with a house, carpets, furniture, and so on. He would even seek nancial help from his parents after his marriage.

Thirdly, if parents do not discriminate between their son and daughter, and if they treat their son-in-law kindly, the son-in-law would often be more helpful to them at times of difculties and is usually more faithful to them in comparison to their own son.

Anyway, is it a woman's fault if she gives birth to a girl? The man and wife are both involved in the action of procreation and a man has no right to blame his wife for this matter. Otherwise it is just as reasonable for a woman to blame her husband in this regard. However, neither are to be blamed, as it is only the will of Allah to determine the sex of a baby.

There are some experts who believe that the sex of a child can be determined from the fact as to how the mother is fed during the rst two months of pregnancy. So if there are people who prefer a particular sex of a baby, they should get in contact with the experts and thus prevent a situation of blaming their wives.

An intellectual man, not only should not upset at having a baby daughter, but must be very happy too. He should show his happiness, should express his affection towards his wife and should even give her a present.

He could celebrate the new birth and even take logical steps in convincing his wife that a baby daughter is just as good as a baby boy, should she be upset with having a daughter.

A wise father would not discriminate between his son and daughter, would not condemn any body for having a daughter, and thus would ght the ignorant concepts of the 'Age of Ignorance'.

"A man heard the news of having a newly born baby daughter, while he was in the presence of the Holy Prophet (S) of Islam. He became upset. The Prophet (S) stated:

'Why are you upset?' He said: 'When I was coming out of my house, my wife was having labour pain, and now they have brought the news to me that I have had a daughter'. The Prophet (S) stated: 'The earth has enough room for her, and the sky provides her with shelter, and Allah will provide her with sustenance. She is a sweet smelling ower from which you will get much enjoyment.'"[259]

Pregnancy and Childbirth

The duration of pregnancy is a very sensitive and fateful period in a baby's life. The mother's nutritional habits together with her physical movements and psychological behavior are vital both to herself and the life of the baby in her womb.

The baby's health or illness, strength or weakness, ugliness and beauty, and its good or bad behavior and a part of intellect and prudence, are established in the mother's womb. One of the experts writes: "The baby's parents are able to either grow in a fortress of

---

[259] Ibid, p 101

health or in the ruins of sickness. It is obvious that the latter is not a suitable place in which the eternal soul or a human being should live. This is the reason that-parents are believed to shoulder the greatest responsibility compared to the whole of creation.'"[260]

Therefore, the period of pregnancy cannot be regarded or be treated as an ordinary one. Once the pregnancy starts, the parents are given a great responsibility.

Parents may unwittingly create a variety of difculties, many of which may be extremely difcult to remedy, because of slight carelessness when performing their duties.

Below are a few points that should be noted:

Food: A foetus in its mother's womb feeds and grows on the nourishment in her blood. Therefore, the mother's food should be nutritive enough to provide the elements needed by the baby as well as for the welfare of the mother. Therefore any lack of vitamins, proteins, fat, sugar or carbohydrates in the mother's intake of food would inict harm on the baby's health.

"Imam as-Sadiq (a.s) stated: 'The food of a foetus, is provided by the nourishment that the mother receives.'"[261]

A major problem which confronts most of the pregnant women is that during either the whole or the majority of the pregnancy period, they lack a well-balanced appetite for food, as they develop craving for certain foods while being repulsed by others. Because they generally eat less, during this period, they should make sure that their food is not stodgy and at the same time nutritious enough to provide the essentials for the baby.

Following up a food program in this phase of pregnancy is extremely difcult, particularly for those of low income and those who are unaware

---

[260] Raz-e-Afrinish, p 108

[261] Bihar al-Anwar, vol 60, p 342

of the nutritional values of different foods.

A great responsibility rests with the father who should do his utmost to provide essential foods for his wife. Carelessness on the part of the father would be harmful to the growing baby, for which he would be held responsible in both this world and in the world Hereafter.

Mental State: A mother, in her pregnancy, needs serenity and should experience a sense of love towards life. This is benecial to both the mother and her baby. The father, being responsible for providing his wife with a peaceful and lively atmosphere, should try even harder during the period of her pregnancy. The husband, through kindness and love, should behave in such a manner that his wife can feel proud and happy about being pregnant; she should feel proud that another life depends on her and that she is responsible for its welfare.

Refrain from Jerky Movements: A pregnant woman should avoid strenuous activities and should rest a great deal. The lifting of heavy objects or fast body movements could result in irreparable harm to her, the baby or both. Pregnant women should refrain from doing any heavy work, and their husbands should volunteer to carry out such activities.

The Fear of Labour: Delivering a baby is not always an easy event. Labour pains can sometimes be severe. Pregnant women often worry about the pain involved and the possible risks associated with child birth, followed by the period of convalescence after giving birth. Although women should be able to cope with pregnancy, labour and feeding their babies, men should also share in the responsibility of bringing up their children.

Although an embryo is conceived in women's womb, there is also the father of the baby who has played an important role in its conception. So men should make certain for their wives' comfort during child birth and be handy if anything should be urgently required.

It is both an Islamic and a human duty of husbands to do their utmost for their pregnant wives to provide medical care and facilities for an easy delivery. A man should try to be with his wife after the birth of their child; but if unable to do so, he should phone her or send a relative to stay with her. He should try to bring her back home himself and help her with the housework so that she can get sufcient rest to regain her lost energy. A man, who treats his wife well, will be rewarded by Allah.

"The Prophet of Allah (S) stated: 'The best of men is one who treats his wife well and I, amongst you, am the best man with regard to the good treatment of my wife.'"[262]

"Imam as-Sadiq (a.s) stated: 'May Allah bless a man who creates a good relationship with his wife, because Allah has appointed man to be the guardian of his wife.'"[263]

A man, who treats his wife well, will make the atmosphere of his family life warmer and will strengthen its foundations.

His wife, in turn, would never forget her husband's love and affection. As a result the bonds of matrimony become stronger.

Assistance in Bringing up Children

A child is the fruit of a marriage. Both man and woman have played a part in his creation and must share in all the difculties and happiness involved. Bringing up a child is a duty for both parents and not only the mother. Although mothers most often take care of their children and attend to their feeding, cleanliness, etc, the fathers should not take their efforts granted. It is not proper for a man to assume that looking after children is a duty for women only and that men have no responsibilities in this matter. It is not fair that a father should leave

---

[262] Wasa'il al-Shi'ah, vol 14, p 122

[263] Ibid

his wife with their crying baby and go to rest in a separate room.

Dear brother! Your child is your responsibility too. Do you think it is fair to leave your wife with a crying baby while you rest in a separate room? Is this the proper way of doing things in your house? Just as you work hard outside the house, your wife works hard inside it, and she needs her sleep just as much as you do yours. She, too, does not enjoy from a screaming baby but she perseveres.

My brother! Humanity as well as Islam demands you to help your wife in bringing up your child. You should either help each other simultaneously or take it in turns.

If your wife experiences a sleepless night and falls asleep after the morning prayer, then you should not expect her to prepare your breakfast like on other days. In fact you should prepare your own and even leave hers ready and waiting for her when she wakes up.

Your wife is not duty-bound to look after your child all the time that you are out of the house or on a trip. In brief, you should assist your wife and share in looking after the child. In this way your family life would be strengthened.

Finally women should also remember that their husbands work hard to earn their living and should not expect them to offer assistance beyond their capacity. Women should not expect their tired, work-weary husbands to begin looking after the children as soon as they return home from work.

The Major Obstacle in Settling down Disagreements

The biggest obstacle in solving family rows are self-centeredness and self-conceit. Unfortunately, many people are affected by these characteristics. Such people lack a certain intelligence whereby they only acknowledge their own virtues while dismissing those of others and never own their failures. It is especially disastrous when this disorder of character is accomplished by another. namely picking up faults with others. Sometimes both husband and wife suffer with the latter in which case they may have a row day and night. Each criticizes the other while tracing themselves totally from all faults.

Sometimes if only one side suffers from this defect of fault-nding, they would pick up fault with the other and by so doing liberate themselves completely from all criticisms.

Where both husband and wife suffer with this disorder, it is particularly difcult to reconcile them, because they would not he prepared to take anyone's advice. When each no listens to the radio or watches a program on television pertaining to family affairs, they would notice a particular ow of character which existed in their partner and would throw it in their faces. But any talked about fault pertaining to themselves would evade their attention. They would buy a book on family morals and hand it over to their partner, without feeling any need for themselves to read it.

Selshness can become so severe that the affected person may not even be aware of it. In such a situation, the relationship between the couple becomes strained and even impossible to continue. Consequently, either life would go on in the form of rows, distress and unhappiness, or may even lead to a divorce.

It is, therefore, recommended to all couples to abstain from selshness and self-conceit. A couple, who are troubled with this situation, should nd time to sit together and like two honest judges talk about their problem(s). They should listen to each other without prejudice. Each one should take a note of his own shortcomings without overlooking even the smallest issue, and with the intention of correcting them.

Then they should both decide to correct themselves; but only if they feel the necessity for deep understanding and where they both long to revive their love and tranquility which once existed between them.

However, in the case of an inability to achieve reconciliation, they should refer their problem(s) to an experienced, faithful, aware, trustworthy, and benevolent person. If such a person is a friend or a relative, it may be to their advantage because they can tell them everything and await their verdict. They should listen to him and take note of his advice given and intend to put it into practice.

Of course being faithful to the recommendations of a judge is not easy, but a person, who is concerned about his family and its stability, peace, and survival, should persevere and later enjoy its valuable results.

Parents of such couples, if aware of their children's family problem(s), should advise them to call on an experienced, faithful, and good intentioned judge. Parents should not take sides with either husband or wife. In this way, with the help of Allah their problems would be resolved.

Allah states in the Holy Qur'an:

> *"And if you fear a breach between the two, then appoint a judge from his people and a judge from her people; if they both desire agreement, Allah will effect harmony between them; surely Allah is Knowing, Aware." (The Holy Qur'an, 4:35)*

Divorce

Although divorce is a lawful act, it is the most detested and worst of all deeds.

"Imam as-Sadiq (a.s) stated: 'Get married but do not divorce, because a divorce would tremble the Arsh (empyrean) of Allah.'"[264]

"Imam as-Sadiq (a.s) also stated: 'Allah likes the house which is inhabited in the wake of marriage and dislikes the house which is

---
[264] Makarim al-Akhlaq, p 225

abandoned in the wake of divorce. There is nothing more detestable to Allah than a divorce.'"²⁶⁵

Marriage is not like buying a pair of shoes and socks that whenever not liked one disposes the shoes and buys another pair of shoes. Marriage is a spiritual covenant that two people make in order to stay together like friends, sympathizers and lovers till their death. It is based on these great hopes that a young girl leaves her parents and joins her husband.

A man makes efforts and works hard on the basis of such a divine covenant. He pays for his wedding and buys the necessary goods for his new life and works for his family comfort.

Marriage is not a lustful affair and a couple cannot destroy it for trivial excuses. Although divorce is lawful, it is seriously detested and people are recommended to avoid it as much as possible.

Unfortunately, this very detestable act has become so common in Islamic countries and the foundations of family units have become so shaky that there is generally little faith in marriage any more.

Divorce is permitted but only in very exceptional and compelling circumstances.

"The Prophet of Allah (S) stated: *Jibrail*(Gabriel) advised me about women so much that I thought one should not divorce them except if they commit adultery.'"²⁶⁶

Most cases of divorce are not based upon good reasons, but are on immature excuses. That is. the reasons for most cases of divorce are trivial and are not worth effecting the separation of a couple. The husband or wife, because of selshness, may exaggerate a trivial problem and decide that their married life must be ended.

"Mrs…, twenty-four years old, asked her husband to invite her

---

²⁶⁵ Wasa'il al-Shi'ah, vol 15, p 267

²⁶⁶ Makarim al-Akhlaq, p 248.

parents to an expensive dinner. Since he did not accept her demand, she applied for a divorce.'"267

"A man divorced his wife on the grounds that she was only giving birth to girls. The couple had five daughters."268

"A woman applied for a divorce, because her husband believes in mysticism and did not show much interest in life."269

"A man applied for a divorce because he wanted to get married to a wealthy woman."270

"A woman applied for a divorce because her husband used to hide his money in his sleeves."271

"A man has divorced his wife because he claims that she is a bad-omen. Since their marriage his father had died and his uncle had become bankrupt."272

A couple who is not wise and prudent, might fall into the traps of such petty matters and apply for a divorce.

A couple, who seeks separations, must not rush for it. They are recommended to consider carefully about the after-effects and their future in detail and then decide. They must specially ponder over two points:

First Point: A couple, who seeks divorce, generally would like to re-marry. But they should remember that after the divorce, the persons known as divorcees would not have a good record with regard to marriage. People think of them as selfish and unfaithful.

Upon finding out a man's previous marriage and divorce, a woman

---

[267] Ittela'at, 12th Esfand, 1350 Solar Hijri.

[268] Ibid, 16th Esfand, 1350 Solar Hijri

[269] Ibid

[270] Ibid, 8th Esfand, 1350 Solar Hijri

[271] Ibid, 16th Esfand, 1350 Solar Hijri

[272] Ibid, 25th Dey, 1350 Solar Hijri

might doubt his faithfulness or his character.

A divorced woman rarely gets a chance to re-marry. Because men generally do not show much interest in marrying a divorced woman and doubt about her faithfulness. Therefore a divorcee would possibly have to stay alone for the rest of his or her life and may have to suffer from loneliness too.

Being lonely is a very difcult situation, and some lonely people prefer death rather than such an unbearable life.

"A twenty-two year old woman who was divorced, attempted to commit suicide on the night of her sister's wedding. She had one child."[273]

Even if a man is successful in re-marrying, it is not at all obvious that his new life would be any better than his rst wife. She may even be worse. Such men usually prefer to divorce their second wife and re-marry the initial one. But usually it is too late for such a move.

"An eighty-year old man said in the court: 'I had a good life when I married my rst wife about sixty years ago. But after a while she started mistreating, so I divorced her. I married a few women after that, but felt that my rst wife was the most faithful among them. I found her and asked her to re-marry me. She, who was also tired of loneliness, agreed, and we now want to marry again.'"[274]

"A man divorced his second wife because she could not take care of the two children that he had from his rst marriage. He than remarried his rst wife whom he had divorced ve years ago."[275]

Second Point: A couple, which seeks separation. Must also think of their children. Children's comfort lies in a family where their both the parents live together and take care of them jointly.

---

[273] Ibid, 17th Esfand, 1348. Solar Hijri.

[274] Ibid, 21st Bahman, 1348 Solar Hijri.

[275] Ibid, 8th Dey, 1348, Solar Hijri

Upon the breaking down of the family life. Children become extremely upset. If only their father looks after them, they would be deprived of motherly love. They would not enjoy life with step-mother either. Step-mothers, not only are unable to act as their genuine mothers but may regard their step-children as a burden. Some step-mothers maltreat their step-children and make them upset deliberately and their fathers may have to remain silent.

"A fourteen-year old bride who had attempted to commit suicide said in the hospital. 'My parents separated when I was one-year old. My father remarried after one and half years and we are now living together. My step-mother used to beat me up and even burnt me with a hot metal rod on a few occasions. My father, even though a well-off man, prevented me from studying and deprived me from learning. About a month ago my father forced me to marry a forty-ve year old man.'"[276]

"A thirteen-year old girl hung herself. This girl lived with her two brothers. One of the brothers said: 'My parents separated about three years ago. My mother re-married another man, and my father died two months ago. It was 6:30 pm yesterday that I came home and found my sister who had hung herself."[277]

Also, if the mother assumes the responsibility of her children, then they would be deprived of having a real father who would care for them. A step-father is often the cause of much unhappiness to his step-children.

"A woman helped her second husband to tie his eight-year old step-son to a bed. They then closed the door and went out for a walk. When they returned home, they found their child had been burnt to death as

---

[276] Kayhan, 29th Aban, 1348 Solar Hijri

[277] Ittela'at, 4th Bahman, 1351 Solar Hijri

a result of the re in the house."²⁷⁸

Divorce destroys a family unit and leaves the children wandering and shelter less. Children often suffer as the result of their parent's selshness.

"Four children aged twelve, nine, six and four years went to a police station. The eldest son said: 'Our parents separated from each other a while ago. They had constant arguments and used to have a row everyday and night. Now that they are divorced, neither are prepared to take the responsibility of caring for us.'"²⁷⁹

Children, who are deprived of having a suitable guardian and a family atmosphere, often go astray. The lack of proper education and a sympathetic person in their lives, makes them suffer from complexes of interiority. They may even commit crimes of various degrees, during their childhood or adulthood.

One can realize this fact by just reading the events in the daily newspapers.

"In a research made at the Center for Youth Rehabilitation, it is evident that out of one hundred and sixteen criminal youths of this center, eighty people asserted that their step-mothers' treatment with them was the cause of their crimes.'"²⁸⁰

Dear madam/sir! For the sake of Allah and for the sake of your innocent children, be forgiving towards each other. Do not exaggerate trivial problems and do not persist in your arguments. Do not pick up faults with each other. Think of your future as well as that of your children.

Remember! Your children rely on you and look up to you for their happiness. Have mercy upon them and do not destroy their lives.

---

[278] Ibid, 18th Bahman, 1348 Solar Hijri.

[279] Ibid, 7th Khurdad, 1349 Solar Hijri

[280] Ibid, 22nd Esfand, 1350 Solar Hijri

If you ignore their internal desires and if you break their little hearts, you would not be able to escape the effects of their unhappiness. You would, therefore, be unable to have a comfortable life together.

www.ingramcontent.com/pod-product-compliance
Lightning Source LLC
LaVergne TN
LVHW041932070526
838199LV00051BA/2787